The Potager Gardener

Plating Your Table with Ingredients You Grow

By Katie Namet

MOUNTAIN PAGE PRESS

Hardback
ISBN: 978-1-952714-57-3
Paperback
ISBN: 978-1-952714-59-7

Editor: Brenda Dammann
Book Design: Wendy Lou Billings

This is a work of creative non-fiction. All of the events in this memoir are true to the best of the author's memory.

Printed in The United States by Ingram Content Group

Publisher
Mountain Page Press
Hendersonville, NC
www.MountainPagePress.com

MOUNTAIN
PAGE PRESS

To my Grandma Mary, who taught me at an early age that love—added to any recipe in life—will always make it taste sweeter.

My Grammy, Mary Bremer
1892-1987

photo circa 1980

Table of Contents

Foreword

There are places we travel to that forever heighten our love of beauty. There are exciting experiences we have which permanently enrich and shape the course of our lives. And there are people we meet who forever raise the quality of our lives and our human experience.

This is the case with my friend, the author of this book. In this loving homage to her people, the earth, and the things that fill life with flavor, contentment, and joy, she celebrates life and the riches of living and creating. When you are with her, or at her table, you feel the senses of joy, laughter, profound satiety of spirit, inspiration, and the gladness of being alive. You know that all life matters, especially yours. For everything she creates and touches with her sincerity and her whole-hearted being, she celebrates you, the earth, and this world. And, magically, she teaches you about celebrating, too, especially you.

Trish Byerly

Acknowledgments

Someone once said, "To have a garden is to believe in tomorrow."

Every day I walk in gratitude for the beauty and sustainability that Creator and Mother Earth provide for us. The Earth's constant cycles of regeneration create an ecosystem of perfect harmony. I am thankful for the chance to live within the magic of this experience, embracing and enhancing my surroundings, and hopefully leaving a smaller carbon footprint in my lifetime.

This book encompasses many roads, each of which led me to this moment. It began with my European ancestors, whose bravery and skills paved their direction as they worked to sustain their families while honoring the Earth. I honor them today and am grateful for the knowledge, history, and wisdom they imparted.

Writing this book helped me remember so many memories, including childhood recollections of my grandparents. I dedicated this book to my ever-so-sweet grandmother, Mary Bremer, in gratitude for her life teachings and her love of kitchen gardening. She showed me how nurturing and loving what we do enhances what we create and who we can become, sharing joy in our daily lives.

What is life without laughter and joy? I am sometimes in awe of the friendships I have, both past and present. These friends continue to support my "scathingly brilliant ideas" while keeping the channel of fun and creativity open for me. Friends enhance the experiences in life, making a simple day colorful.

Trish Byerly is one of those friends, offering daily doses of fun energy and insight which ground those ideas. Her limitless support and graciousness have given me the freedom to expand and try new recipes and ideas. Sharing this book experience with her has made this a fun journey for me. I am grateful to her and her family for all the love and support they've given.

Every endeavor always has a beginning point. That beginning point for me was a journal my dear friend Marsha Stephenson gave to me as a present during the Covid crisis, a time when I was secluded with more time than usual. As I began recalling and writing down my childhood memories, the journal evolved into an idea, which then evolved into this book. I will always be grateful for that launching point, which led me here. Marsha shares an infectious laugh and sense of adventure while always providing the perfect support, whether sitting on a tractor or cooking together. I am grateful for her generous encouragement, along with that of her most precious husband, Joe, and her loving family who always welcomes me.

I have had the most spectacular support from my publishing company, Mountain Page Press. Putting together this book from start to finish has been a lovely experience. When I first spoke with my publisher, Sam Nace, I felt a kindred spirit…the kind of feeling you get when you've been friends with someone for a long time. Her knowledge and joy for her profession continued throughout the process, keeping me organized with timelines and direction. Her lovely spirit is always cheerful and dynamic, making this experience a happy one. I'll always be in awe of her ability to switch business hats, and I will always be grateful for the opportunity she provided me.

Now, Mountain Page Press comes with a dynamic staff of people…so many wonderful people, each of whom had a hand in helping to make this book be the best it can be. Editors, proofreaders, designers, and a host of behind-the-scenes book angels I didn't even have the pleasure of meeting personally. Know that you're appreciated! I am grateful for editor Brenda Dammann, who continued to dig deeper into my family history, and pushed me to expand beyond my boundaries! Her dedication to the story inspired me, and her uncanny ability to know what wanted to be expressed, every step of the way, was brilliant.

I hope this book inspires each reader to continue exploring and experimenting with a potager garden and connecting more deeply to Mother Earth. My hope for you is to creatively make your garden space work for you, while strengthening sustainability in your part of the world.

Remember your "roots"!

Katie Thamert

THE *Potager* GARDENER

Introduction

How many ingredients can you grow? In the old country, my great- and great-great-grandparents planted for their family's survival. They preserved food, kept a root cellar, and produced a winter garden. Generations later my grandparents settled in America, and even though their life was very different, it was still intimately tied to growing food. They planted row after row of one or two crops, like corn, wheat, or soybeans. They sold at the farmers' exchange and grain mills. My grandfather farmed for the Campbell Soup company, which provided a living for his family.

My grandparents were a constant presence in my life. They canned in the winter and cooked huge meals for the family. They were teachers of love, and their respect for the earth melded into everyday life, a quiet but mindful manner that enveloped you the minute you crossed their doorstep. Rooms were filled with scents of freshly picked flowers and a table full of inviting food. Everything was so welcoming and created a rhythm to life that made sense, especially to me, as a young child.

Compassion and care for all living things permeated my grandparents' home inside and out, with rooms full of colorful flowers and plants that were lovingly tended. Dehydrated herbs hung in the kitchen and smelled divine. My memories of that childhood time still linger today. I can taste the past on my tongue and feel the traditions by which they lived.

I can still picture their home clearly. Celebrations and holidays, especially Christmas, would unfold in their home, and seemed as if they could last days or weeks. Preparations were always completed before you arrived: Christmas trees were trimmed outside with lights, and a homemade spruce wreath hung on the door with a crisp bow. Inside was a dining room table that, as a child, seemed as if it could feed entire families, communities, or even kingdoms. Grandma was only four foot ten, but she was a giant in the kitchen. The smells of her cooking magically and instantly enveloped you. You knew that so much was in the making because of love—her love for us—and her passion for creating culinary magic for the table. Her nonstop smiling and humming added a special touch to every dish.

Grandma's aprons were starched and pressed, conveying that there was serious business happening in that kitchen. She was a master chef who never used a recipe, the measurements and ingredients locked up tight in the vault of her mind. Baking was her forte. Bread, sweet rolls, cakes, pies, biscuits—you name it, she made it like no one else could. When we visited, her table looked like a European bakery. She crafted everything by hand; the only appliance she had was a toaster. Her knives were worn down from continual use and Grandpa's sharpening.

I remember so many details from when I was a young girl: sights, smells, sounds, flavors, and things I could touch. Ceramic crocks held fragrant sauerkraut and other delicious treasures. Mason jars lined a

long cabinet wall, filled with tomatoes, jam, pickles, relishes—arranged more beautifully than any framed art or sculpture. Even though Grandpa made pickles in crocks, Grandma made "backups" in jars, chasing after the perfect recipe, each of which were so different and wonderful.

Grandpa was proud of his garden, too. He grew organic produce long before it was a fashionable label at grocery stores. His thumb was so green I sometimes wondered if a witch in the forest hadn't given him magic beans. Everything he touched grew to abundance and perfection. I was always excited to explore plum trees, gardens, and flowers, finding which new plants had appeared since my last visit.

I remember a pile of seed catalogs and a *Farmer's Almanac* next to my grandfather's oversized chair. Since 1793, the annual *Farmer's Almanac* publication guided the farming season with year-long anecdotal weather prognostications, planting schedules, and sundry pleasantries of rural interest. He sorted through seed catalogs all winter, looking for new and favorite varieties, dreaming of what he could plant in the spring. It was always a miracle to me how his tiny seeds became a Garden of Eden each year.

The way they lived was taught to me by example, and every lesson came with a story. In one of my first memories, around the age of five, I tagged along as Grandma tended the roses. I wanted to help, and she said I could water them when she was done pruning. She told me, "Roses like their feet wet and their heads dry." Now, I don't know if it's true, and maybe it doesn't matter, but I learned that the way she moved through the garden made me feel happy to participate. To this day, I still believe this is the best way to care for my roses.

My parents lived in Chicago, where they had a garden in the yard and grew rows of tomatoes along with a few other vegetables. With the invention of freezers, much of what they grew was preserved and used in soups and stews. In a new world of industrial convenience, they even cooked and froze meals ahead of time to make mealtime easier for their busy city family. Farm to table and everything in between—that was the rhythm of life. Enjoying and sharing the fruits of their labor created a life of abundance; it was how I learned that loving what you do becomes loving who you are.

Looking back on my childhood, I realize I've always had a connection to the rhythm of nature. My ancestors understood the seasonal cycles and connected to that harmony. They were biodynamic farmers, following the cycles of the moon and the seasons for planting, cultivating, and harvesting. My grandparents had a circadian rhythm to their life, with early hours that matched the needs a homestead required. I, too, feel that connection to the cycles. There's a primal understanding of timing, and an innate feeling of "knowing." Maybe it's generational survival instincts that all come back to me now, instincts from the multitude of ancestors who came before me.

How many ingredients can you grow? This wasn't a question I consciously asked myself. But as an adult, I began to crave a simpler lifestyle. As an organic vegetarian, I wanted fresh foods, not frozen or canned. Canned foods lose one-third of vitamins A and C. Frozen foods also lose their nutrients over time and, if they're not eaten quick enough, risk freezer burn. After growing up in a family who gardened, canned, and made incredible food, I was destined to eventually follow in their footsteps. I set out trying to recreate their recipes, traditions, and ideas.

The effort left me humbled and inspired. My grandma and mother cooked by feel, never with measurements, so I also learned how to cook by feel from them. Growing my own food and "shopping" from my garden allowed me to access fresh, organic ingredients, gathering only what I needed for my recipes. In addition, I now eat and live differently than my grandparents, so their recipes have been adapted for modern life. For me, that meant a bigger variety of herbs and vegetables instead of an abundance of rows growing many of the same. The mixture of flowers, fruit borders, scented herbs, and colorful vegetables offers a healthier and a more complete aesthetic to my garden.

But I saw how life could be if we learned to live so fully on so little. Looking at why my grandparents planted their garden, and knowing how they used each plant from root to flower following the seasonal cycle, I felt deeply connected to their experience. It gave me a new perspective of how the past informs our present and makes us more aware of our natural rhythms.

Over the course of this book, I'll share what I've learned and challenge others to grow what they eat, be it from a balcony of potted herbs, vegetables, and fruits or a large yard with a massive garden.

By planting with purpose, all the recipes in this book are possible to create from a garden of any scale. Develop your own touch, eat with the seasons, and be inspired to make your own traditions. You'll be surprised to discover how using what you have is always enough. I want you to enjoy the journey as much as I have. I hope this book—and your potager garden—encourages you to live more independently, leave a smaller carbon footprint, and make your own traditions for future generations.

My Gardening Story

I came from a long background of generational farmers, so when I thought about starting my own garden, I envisioned rows and rows of crops on big tracts of land. I thought about all that work—the planting, the harvesting, all the weeds! And what would I do with bundles and bundles of vegetables as a household of one? It was intimidating.

But there came a time when I needed to be healthier, to enhance my diet, and have readily available organic vegetables and herbs. But when I started changing the way I ate in the late '80s and early '90s, being "organic" was really limiting; there were few choices available at the market for a complete diet. I started to think about growing my own, but I was intimidated by what I thought the normal garden would be. Despite these misgivings, I continued to feel drawn to the idea for many reasons: it was about making better use of my time, it was about faith, and it was about my health. It was always important to me to eat living foods.

I always favored aesthetically beautiful backyards which showcased lots of flowers in various stunning arrays. This is the type of garden that always stuck with me. But then I remembered the kitchen garden that Grandma had—a potager garden—which was typically right outside the kitchen door. You could grow your vegetables, herbs, flowers, and fruit, grabbing what you needed for each meal. I realized I didn't have to plant rows and rows of carrots; a small "kitchen" garden would allow me to plant any quantity I wanted.

This idea of a potager kitchen garden was less intimidating, and I loved how malleable it was—I could harvest a lettuce leaf here, a tomato there. I learned I could plant things in a way that created a beautiful, edible landscape. I didn't need bushels of things or some huge garden in the "back 40" that required hours of work each week.

The potager garden also allowed me to harvest continuously, an aspect I came to love. With prior thinking, there was something to harvest every day. So, out of a sense of need, I created a potager garden. I then became slowly more creative, adding those elements which made it the perfect space for me. It became a place to sit and meditate, a place I used as part of everyday life.

Now I feel drawn to my garden—connected, peaceful, relaxed. It's a quiet space. My take on my garden is that I can walk out there and make a new dish every day from what's waiting for me in the soil.

"Now I feel drawn to my garden—connected, peaceful, relaxed. It's a quiet space."

What Is a Potager Garden?

In French "potager" refers to a kitchen garden, which is what my grandmother grew. But the history behind planting a potager garden is both humbler and grander than that. Potager gardens combined the utility of a simple, purposeful vegetable plot with intricate garden designs containing patterns laid out in quadrants with pathways around the beds. Most often laid close to the kitchen, the French cultivated these gardens with ornamental flowers mixed in with herbs, vegetables, and fruit trees. Decorative trellises or bushes were sometimes used to line the beds or paths, with a central focal point of benches, topiaries, sculptures, or fountains.

The History of Potager Gardens

The tradition of potager gardening goes back to Roman times when kitchen gardens were laid out in ornate geometric patterns called "castra." Today, many French gardens retain the form and style of these ancient gardens, such as the *parterre de broderie* or "embroidery pattern" garden, inspired by embroidery motifs.

In later centuries, the concept developed and expanded beyond the kitchen garden to include formal geometric gardens with extensive paths or borders that made elaborate designs when viewed from above. During the Renaissance in France, these geometric gardens became associated with power and nobility because only wealthy landowners could afford to create them. Ornate gardens like these still exist today.

You can still find some extensive potager gardens in France. These typically have the practical aspects of terracing, irrigation systems, and raised beds to support vegetables. They also retain many of the traditional aesthetic features, such as French parterres with hedges and paths, flower beds, and decorative statuary.

Today, potager gardens are still designed to be as beautiful and ornamental as they are utilitarian, often continuously planted to remain productive year-round. Whether freeform and whimsical or formal and architectural in structure, every potager garden is as beautiful as it is functional. In this way, potager gardens beautify a space and bring food to the table.

Traditional Potager Garden Design

A potager garden is not just a place to grow food; it can also be a work of art. A very traditional design for a potager garden has multiple levels of raised beds interspersed with gravel pathways and mixed borders and hedges surrounding the garden. Potager gardens are often laid out at angles rather than straight lines to create an appealing view from above. Typically, you will find a focal point such as an ornamental statue or birdbath at the center of the layout, acting as a reference point for the entire design.

The common elements in most potager gardens include:

- A focal point of some kind such as a statue, birdbath, or pond
- Decorative features such as arbors, trellises, and pedestals
- Paths made from materials such as gravel, flagstone, or earth
- Terracing for larger gardens
- Herbs that include rosemary, thyme, and lavender
- Beds, often with raised borders, to support annual vegetables such as tomatoes, beans, and peas
- Roses and other flowers
- Various fruit trees or fruit borders

Potager garden design is not restricted to rectangular beds. In fact, some gardeners choose to plant circular or triangular beds that still fit within the general definition of a potager design. I'm big on recycling, so if you've got an old ladder to put pots on, use it! Add a bench, rocks, a set of wind chimes, whatever you have.

There are also several different styles of potager gardens that you can create, each with its own set of unique characteristics. You can use any style to achieve the goal of having an attractive food garden. These include:

- Edible landscapes
- Vertical gardens
- Herb spirals
- Vegetable trellises

If there is ample space, multiple elements can be used simultaneously to create a visually appealing and useful garden. Small gardens can easily get away with using just one or two of these elements.

Your Own Potager Garden

We really need to make a concentrated effort to bring a variety of quality, organic food back into our lives. Regardless of lack of space, time, or knowledge, anybody can garden in any space, whether it be a rooftop, a balcony, or a small or large backyard.

The first thing you need to realize is there's no right or wrong way to grow a potager garden. Make it as big or small as you choose, as elaborate or simple as you want. Add layers with different flowers, companion plants for bug protection, and decorative items. Once you have your garden, use it as you need—just a few beans or a single lettuce leaf at a time if you want.

You can sustain yourself from your backyard with very little effort; you don't have to depend on what's happening "out there." Unlike the food at grocery stores, this produce comes from your own balcony or backyard. As such, you have full control of what goes into it—it's all up to you.

Traditional gardens today are typically located away from the house, planted in straight lines, and entirely practical. There are few aesthetic features other than (maybe) some flowers surrounding the vegetable plots. In contrast, a potager garden is created from the start to be aesthetically pleasing and placed near the kitchen for easy use. I love the idea of an edible landscape.

Your own potager garden can be flexible. Use a corner of your yard. Plant in raised beds with paths in between. Or plant in pots on a small balcony if you don't have yard space. Anything can make the perfect potager garden! But the most important feature is to create a usable garden, with plants—including edible flowers and herbs—for recipes your heart desires. In any form, the potager garden is perfect for the organic kitchen gardener who wants to challenge themselves to grow as much of the food they consume as possible.

Plant what you love to eat, first and foremost. But keep in mind that potager gardens are not just for vegetables! Consider planting some favorite flowers, too. Plant some for the butterflies, or maybe try some edible flowers. Are you allergic to strawberries? Plant blueberries or raspberries in containers.

A potager garden can also reflect who you are beyond the food you want to eat. Incorporate a sense of magic into your garden by the way you choose to design the space, what to plant, and how to decorate. You can plant herbs that are not only good additions to the food you cook, but also contain medicinal or spiritual properties. Use rocks or crystals as meaningful focal points, or choose a garden statue important to your life or spiritual path. Imagine your garden as a site where the spirits of the land—like the Irish sidhe or fae folk—come alive and gather.

Visualize the garden's seasonal cycles as they correlate to the Greek myth of Persephone and Demeter. When Hades took Persephone into the underworld, Demeter, the goddess of all growing things, mourned the loss of her daughter. In her grief, all plant life died, and the earth became barren. It wasn't until the gods agreed that Persephone could spend half the year with Demeter and half with Hades that the earth began to bloom again in the spring. When Persephone returned to the underworld, winter came, and the earth once again grew fallow.

In today's culture, we take the ready availability of fruits and vegetables for granted in many ways, disconnecting us from nature's cycles. But when you grow your favorite foods in a garden, you reconnect to the earth's cycles. What you plant in your potager garden will follow the season's rich bounty spring, summer, and fall. If you're resourceful, your garden can even provide what you need through the winter.

By creating winding, labyrinthine paths, a potager garden can bring up another image from Greek mythology: the story of Theseus and the Minotaur. The real hero of this story wasn't Theseus at all but Princess Ariadne, daughter of King Minos. As Theseus descended into the labyrinth to battle the gruesome minotaur, it was Ariadne who gave him a thread to unwind as he made his way into the labyrinth's deepest places. He then used the thread to find his way back after defeating the minotaur.

In the same way, think of everything you plant in your potager garden as a thread that ties you to nature and the landscape, providing foods that nourish the body and soul while pleasing the eye.

Tips for Starting Your Potager Garden

With so much information out there, the thought of starting your own garden can be intimidating. So many things to consider! So many experts! So very many opinions.

But this is the bottom line: gardening is about melding your desires with your experience, available time, and space. Create the best possible scenario for the outcome you desire. Start where you feel comfortable! Make sure you allow the time required for what you want to accomplish. Anything more—taking on too much—will only result in overwhelm. It's important to keep confusion to a minimum.

Everyone's garden will be different, as we all come to our gardens with various levels of knowledge, experience, and limitation. You may live in a city with limited space, or in a planting zone that provides little time to yield certain produce. Just remember that no matter your situation, all gardens are possible!

Here are a few suggestions before getting started:

Space and Inventory

The first thing to do is evaluate your available space for gardening. Do you have a balcony? Or maybe a rooftop? Maybe you have a backyard or a place on your property that already has remnants of a garden long past. Does a small container garden or a larger potager garden appeal to you?

Inventory what's already there. Are there any trees or bushes bearing nuts or fruits that can be incorporated into the plan? Does your property already have any volunteer plants or wild berry patches? Is there anything you would like to transplant or use in your garden? Are there opportunities to lay out your garden in a decorative way to add beauty to your property?

As far as "design" goes, start simple. What would you like to see as your central focal point? A trellis? A tiny fountain? A mirrorball? Do you want to incorporate raised beds? Can you create pathways with dirt, grass, or flagstone? How can you include decorative elements? While most people envision a potager garden with four quadrants, you can choose any design, from spirals to circles to elaborate patterns.

Sun

Scan your potential garden area. How much sun does the space get every day? Does a privacy fence or a wall block the sun? What about trees or hedges that filter sunlight? A potager garden is typically located right off the kitchen area for convenience, but if that area doesn't provide enough (or too much) sun, you may want to choose a different space, or only grow flowers and vegetables that fit the available sunlight. If you utilize decorative containers or pots, you can arrange them in specific places to catch different amounts of sunlight. Seed packets will always provide valuable information, so start by reading them, familiarizing yourself with how much sun each requires.

Moisture

Having access to water is a necessity for growing a garden, as is knowing the average amount of rainfall your area experiences every year. Too little or too much rainfall makes it a challenge to grow certain plants. The moisture levels in certain parts of the country lend themselves to fungus or blight.

Likewise, being close to an alternate water source is helpful. Having sprinklers or a water connection close by can help if rainfall is scarce during the growing season.

Examine your gardening area: Are you on a slope where water drains off swiftly? Does your space flood, or pool water after a rain? Is there an overhang from the roof that will wash out the area during a rain?

Soil

Whether you are working with raised beds, containers, or a fresh spot in your backyard, you should learn what type of soil you have. Is it rich black loam? Southern red clay? Sand-based? Do you plan on using bagged planting soil from a garden store for an easier start? Or fill dirt, ordered and dropped off by the cubic yard?

To ensure that your garden grows and your vegetables are rich in nutrients, your soil must provide a healthy foundation. Start by purchasing a simple soil test from your area's agriculture extension office or gardening center. Send it in to discover what nutrients may be lacking in your specific soil. Once you locate any deficiencies in your soil, supplement it by adding the recommended nutrients. There are many schools of thought on this, and a wide range of books to guide you; among them, The Old Farmer's Almanac Vegetable Gardener's Handbook.

What to Plant

Deciding what to plant usually comes down to this: what would you most like to eat? Planting vegetables or herbs that you won't use will take space away from the food you love. Don't plant zucchini if you don't like it. Leave out the cilantro if it tastes like soap. Plant what works for you, not just what you think a garden is supposed to have. Emphasize the things you love and focus on the harvest that makes your heart and palate sing.

We've all heard stories of neighbors and family members pawning off bumper crops of overgrown zucchinis and tomatoes. Again, it's important to evaluate your area and the maintenance required before you plant. Understanding the typical yield of each food you plant will help you decide the number of plants you actually need.

Start out by planting small, since it's very easy to yield more than enough to eat as things grow. Beginners may want to focus on something low maintenance, like a pot of garlic or a jute sack of potatoes to build their confidence the first year. Or start with flowers and maybe a container of mixed herbs or lettuce greens. Trellises can be fun for growing pie pumpkins, peas, cucumbers, and squash. If you won't be canning or preserving your yield, planting small amounts leaves room for more varieties, and requires less maintenance.

Another fun subset to investigate is "companion planting"—specific plants you can add in borders and among vegetables to enhance pollination, attract desirable elements, and naturally repel predators and insects. (Find the section on companion planting later in this book.)

The secret to choosing the right seeds is knowing what "planting zone" you are in. The U.S. and Southern Canada are divided into eleven planting zones based on climate and winter temperatures. The U.S. Department of Agriculture has a plant hardiness zone map which serves as the standard for gardening and farming in different parts of the country, so it's also an important resource.

Choosing seeds based on your zone is key. For example, if you live in the north, a heartier tomato is needed to endure the cooler weather and shorter growing season. In the south, you need a tomato that will survive fungus and sustain itself in the heat. After knowing your zone, you can choose your herbs, flowers, fruits, and vegetables. Choosing quality seeds from reputable companies is important for a good yield. Seeds that have been sitting around in a discount store may be old and not germinate. You now have the start of a plan!

Depending on time and interest, there are a few more choices involved while planning out your garden. Do you want to grow from seeds or started plants? Some plants—like carrots—are easy to start from seed in your garden. Other plants can be sourced from nurseries that sell seedlings already started; all you need to do is transplant them in your garden. This is very convenient, but sometimes it can be hard to track down the seedlings for certain varieties of plants.

Other people love the idea of starting their plants inside with grow lights or a greenhouse. When I lived in Michigan, the growing season was shorter than here in North Carolina, so seedlings had to be started inside, then gradually hardened to survive cooler weather. Again, don't take on more than your time or interest allows.

Tools

Whether planting directly in the soil, in a container, or in a raised bed, having the appropriate tools will help your garden flourish as you get started. This list can get extensive, depending on the size of your area and how many gadgets you want. Here's a good starter list:

- A good pair of garden gloves
- Shovel for scooping (sized according to the size of the garden)
- Spade for digging
- Rake
- Pruning tool
- Hand trowel
- Garden hose with adjustable nozzle
- Watering can
- Wheelbarrow or wagon
- Flowerpots or larger container pots
- Basket for gathering items you harvest

Ingredients for the Recipe Master List

When people ask, "How do I decide what to plant in my garden?" there are so many variables. Start by asking what you want to eat. Planting food you don't want is just waste of time.

Another way is to use this cookbook to decide what you want to make, then plan your garden accordingly. Below is the list of herbs, fruits, vegetables, and flowers used for the recipes in this book, which can be a guide in choosing what to plant in your own potager garden. Again: plant what you enjoy eating and start small. Keep in mind that multiple herbs can be combined in a single container (or choose a few favorites to begin).

Take time to compare your available area, ambition, and this list…then plan what you need. Take time to learn about the plants you want to grow. Knowledge will keep you from becoming intimidated and frustrated. You will be surprised what you can do!

Vegetables

Butternut Squash, Cabbage, Carrots, Cauliflower, Cherry Tomatoes, Cobs of Corn, Cucumbers, Eggplant, Garlic, Kale, Napa Cabbage, Onion, Parsnips, Peppers, Plum Tomatoes, Rainbow Swiss Chard, Red Onion, Red Pepper, Spaghetti Squash, Spinach, Sweet Peppers, Sweet Potatoes, White Potatoes, Yellow Squash, Zucchini

Herbs

Basil, Chamomile, Chervil, Chives, Coriander, Cumin, Dill, Fennel Seeds, Lemon Thyme, Mint, Nutmeg, Oregano, Parsley, Pineapple Sage, Rosemary, Sage, Thyme, Turmeric

Fruits

Berries, Cherries, Lemons, Limes, Oranges, Peaches, Pineapple

Flowers

Lavender, Roses, Sunflowers, Violets

I, for one, am always looking for multiple uses for what I plant, and so should you. Use herbs and flowers to change your food and add nutrition. For example, I use herbs for making teas and medicinal products as well as cooking and baking. Dill is one example. I pickle with it, use it in potato salad, and toss it on my lettuce salads. Basil isn't just for pesto—I mix it into sauces and garnish salads with it. If you're going to plant a flower, plant flowers that you can eat—put them in your salads, make them into a garnish, or infuse them in your honey. Some herbs are also flowering, like lavender, for instance. You can display it, cook and bake with it, and make soaps, scents, skin toners, and facial products. And, of course, flowers can be lovely just to have on your table. There's joy in finding multiple ways to use a harvested flower or herb; it keeps you from getting food fatigue.

You can use many of the same design principles for a flower garden. Perennials, annuals, and bulbs all lend themselves to this type of garden, and the various color schemes can add to your enjoyment. As with a vegetable garden, be sure to incorporate flowers that attract bees or repel pests.

The beautiful design of a potager garden is not difficult to create. All you need is some space, a plan, and the will to carry it out. Pinterest and the internet are great places to find different garden designs and ideas for every size garden.

Edible Flowers

If you're going to plant a flower, plant one you can eat. It's just smart gardening. You can do so much with edible flowers…from savory cooking and sweet baking to gorgeous garnishes. Many people don't explore the idea of edible flowers because they think it's weird to eat them. But you're expanding yourself, your kitchen, and your skill sets. It's exciting!

And if it's still too much to contemplate, you can always make other things like teas, infusions, soaps, and other botanical skin products with them. They're great in drinks. Freeze them in ice cubes for extra decoration. And they're always beautiful as a garnish or in a vase at your table.

I've done all of the above. At one time, I even had a company where I made different teas that included dried fruit, herbs, and edible flowers. Once you start on the path with edible flowers, you can take all kinds of twists and turns.

Potager gardens often incorporate flowers or herbs in flowerpots. I plant them in containers so I can keep them under wraps. And, of course, flowering fruits and vegetables will always be an excellent addition to your garden. Whatever you choose to grow, pick things that you love—whether it's how they look or how they taste.

There are edible decorative flowers, vegetable flowers, and herb flowers. Below are the ones I would love you to consider.

Decorative Edible Flowers

BEGONIA - Leaves, flowers, and stems are edible, with a sour citrus flavor. Petals can be used for salads or garnish.

CALENDULA (Marigolds) - Spicy to peppery flavor. Called the poor man's saffron because of the coloring. Used in rice, soups, pasta dishes, salads. Only petals are edible.

CARNATIONS - Use for desserts, cakes, or candy. The smaller carnation flower (Dianthus) has a nutmeg scent. Used to make Chartreuse, a French liqueur.

CHRYSANTHEMUMS - Colorful, tangy, peppery flavor. Remove the base and use the petals. Leaves are used to flavor vinegar. Blanch and use in stir fry.

CLOVER - Licorice flavor, sweet. Use white clover in salads.

CORNFLOWER - Or as my grandmother called them, bachelor buttons. Spicy-sweet clove flavor. Use in salads, as a garnish, or as a natural food dye.

DANDELION - Honey-sweet flavor. Pick when young and use for wine, salads, or rice.

DAYLILIES - Sweet vegetable flavor. Cut off the base. The sweet petals can be stuffed like squash blossoms or used in desserts.

FUCHSIA - Beautifully shaped flower with bright colors. Edible berries too! Use as a garnish.

GARDEN SORREL - Lemon taste. Use as you would where you use lemon—in salads or sauces.

GLADIOLUS - Remove anthers and use petals on salads or in spreads.

HIBISCUS - Citrus cranberry taste. I dry them and make tea. You can also add them to salads.

IMPATIENS - Pretty little petals that are sweet. Garnish in salads or summer drinks.

JOHNNY JUMP UPS - Purple, white, and yellow blooms. For salads, mixed in soft cheeses, or added to drinks, soups, desserts, and cakes.

LILAC - Floral lemon taste. Used for desserts or crystallizing with sugar for pastries and salads.

NASTURTIUM - Sweet spicy flavor. Leaves have a peppery taste. Use for garnish, in open luncheon sandwiches, or on appetizers.

PANSY - Petals have a mild taste. If the whole flower is eaten, it has a mild wintergreen flavor. Use in fruit salads, soups, desserts, garnishes, and green salads.

ROSES - Sweet, fruity to spicy flavor. Many varieties. Use in desserts, teas, ice cream, salads, party ice cubes, syrups, butter, jelly, garnishes…the list is endless!

VIOLETS - Lovely yellows and purples. Use the tender leaves and flowers in salads, desserts, cakes, or crystallized in sugar. Leaves are edible and can be cooked as you would spinach.

Herb Flowers

ALLIUMS - Leeks, garlic, chives, or garlic chives. All parts are edible. Flowers are more robust in flavor than leaves. Use in salads, soups, or with vegetables.

ANGELICA - Seeds and stems can be candied or used in liqueurs. Use leaves in salads, in teas, or with fish. Celery flavor.

ANISE HYSSOP - Licorice flavor typically used in Asian dishes. Use flowers and leaves as garnish or in salads.

BASIL - Lemon-mint flavor used in salads and pasta dishes.

BEE BALM - Tastes like oregano and mint. Use leaves and petals in salads—fruit salads or green.

BORAGE - Blue star blossoms are cucumber-tasting. Use in cold soups, dips, or punches.

CILANTRO - Flowers have herbal flavor. Use in salads or cold vegetable dishes.

FENNEL - Yellow blossoms with mild anise flavor. Use as garnish, or in desserts or cold soups.

LAVENDER - Sweet, lemony floral taste. For desserts, cakes, stews, ice cream, focaccia, or herb breads.

LEMON VERBENA - Cream-colored citrus flower. Use flowers as tea leaves, or to flavor desserts.

MINT - Use flowers and leaves for tea, drinks, and in Middle Eastern dishes.

OREGANO - Flowers are milder than leaves. Use anywhere you would use the herb.

ROSEMARY - Use blossoms in seafood, Mediterranean dishes, and lemon rosemary dishes.

SAGE - Violet, blue, pink, and white blossoms for salads and garnishes, with mushrooms, or as pesto.

SAVORY - Hot and peppery flavor.

THYME - Use in soups and garnish.

Vegetable Blossoms

ARUGULA - Small white blossoms for use in salads.

RADISH FLOWERS - Yellow, pink, or white for use in salads.

SCARLET RUNNER BEANS - A bright red, tasty garnish for soups and salads.

SQUASH, PUMPKIN, AND ZUCCHINI BLOSSOMS - Remove stamens, stuff with cheese.

Companion Planting

One dynamic aspect of gardening success is "companion planting," or creating a mutually beneficial mix of flowers, vegetables, fruits, and herbs within the gardening space. Companion planting adds beauty and interest to your potager garden, but more importantly, the right combination of plants does so much more:

- Helps protect plants from unwanted insects
- Attracts pollinating insects and birds
- Increases plant productivity
- Improves the flavor of edibles
- Creates an attractive landscape

For example, a flowering annual (such as a zinnia) may attract birds and bees needed for pollination. Another plant may lure harmful insects away from its neighbor (without being harmed itself). Other plants, especially herbs, may completely deter harmful insects altogether. Some companion plants either use similar minerals and nutrients in the soil or replace nutrients (like nitrogen) that other plants deplete. Legume plants can bring nitrogen to the surface. Root vegetables extend deep into the soil and bring other nutrients close, benefitting vegetables and flowers with shallow root systems.

Variability in height and density is another component of companion planting. Plants of varying stature often benefit each other. A fruit tree might provide shade for plants requiring partial sun, for example, or protect smaller neighboring plants from wind and rain. Taller supporting plants grown next to plants with a vine structure—like peas or string beans—can provide trellis support in place of stakes and string. Alternating large and small plants with ground-covering plants helps control unwanted weeds (aka unwanted plants) that would otherwise take root.

Popular Companion Plants

To achieve their various mutual benefits, companion plants should be grown close to each other, and have compatible needs for soil, weather conditions, water, and sunlight. To select the best companion plants for your garden, first check your planting zone to determine the best plants for your region, including native plants. Data from the U.S. Department of Agriculture website also provides information on both beneficial and harmful insects, in addition to current insect infestations in your region.

Many insects, including cabbage moths, are repelled by those varieties of ground cover with beautiful odors like mint, basil, dill, and other herbs. Ground covers such as mint, basil, and sage will grow in most soils. Mint, especially, is one herb that can take over any empty ground.

Beans, onions, peppers, and tomatoes make great companion plants next to carrots.

Rosemary planted nearby will discourage insects while adding flavor to neighboring plants. Basil grown close to tomato and lettuce plants may increase the yield, improving the flavor of lettuce and leafy greens grown within a foot of the plant.

Bright nasturtiums, marigolds, or caper plants add color to a vegetable garden while drawing troublesome nematodes and aphids away from other plants. Nasturtiums and caper flowers are edible, and yield seeds which can be pickled and used as flavorings.

Don't forget the blossoming plants like fruit trees and flowering vegetables, which attract pollinating bees and hummingbirds, along with various other colorful birds. Adding feeders will increase their presence while supporting bird life, creating another layer of enjoyment from your windows.

Garden Design with Companion Plants

You can design your potager garden with circles, rectangles, or any shape compatible with your space and landscaping. Companion plants add so much interest and can be combined anywhere: in a front yard, patio, or backyard garden. Planning a garden with consideration for companion planting will enhance healthy crops and add aesthetic value. When combined with companion plants, the best potager gardens beautify the landscape while providing organically grown edibles.

Rather than sticking with one or two types of plants in your garden, think about adding decorative trees and shrubs, flowers, fruit-based trees and shrubs, vines, and grasses. Take joy in experimenting with the intricacies of companion planting as your skills grow.

Herbs

Herbs are an essential part of any kitchen and a fragrant and lovely part of a potager garden, adding both beauty and practicality. Take the time to learn more about herbs that you can grow in a potager garden. What herbs grow best in your region? Plant herbs that will flourish where you live.

And if you worry, as I have, that you can't use all the herbs right away, dry them or grind them into a powder for use in recipes. Drying and preserving herbs from your potager garden adds variety to your pantry. Herbs—which include basil, marjoram, rosemary, thyme, oregano, mint, chives, sage, parsley, and even peppers—all add great flavor to your recipes. Enjoy the fragrance of the leaves as they dry! Your home will be filled with glorious scents. Keep dried herbs in bottles, plastic packages, or freeze for future use.

Harvesting Herbs

Pick herb leaves and stems in the morning before sun exposure. Carefully discard any that are damaged or imperfect. Use the best leaves for the fullest flavor. Wash the leaves and stems with cold water (sometimes little insects can be underneath). Pat dry on a paper towel.

Drying Herbs

There are several ways to dry herbs, beginning with a food dehydrator. You'll want to invest in a dehydrator; you can use it for so many different garden harvests. Dehydrators allow you to have herbs in abundance during the winter months. You can purchase various units online or at most big box appliance stores.

Set the dehydrator thermostat to 95-155° Fahrenheit. Place herbs on the racks and follow the instructions for the appliance. Do not cut or crush the leaves! They will crumble when they are dried. Check the dehydrator occasionally to see how well they are drying.

Oven Drying

You can also use your oven to dry herbs and enjoy the scents. Set the oven to 115°F. Spread the herbs on a tray or cookie sheet. It will take three or four hours to dry the herbs in your oven. Be sure to check the herbs periodically.

Microwave Drying

In a hurry? Put the herbs on a paper towel. Cover with another towel and dry on low wattage (1000 watts) for two or three minutes. Check the herbs at 30-second intervals.

Air Dry Indoors

This is the best way to air dry in a damp climate; just be aware that it can take a week or more to dry herbs this way. Mint, thyme, sage, and other herbs can be dried using this method. Bunch the herbs and tie the stems with a string, placing them in a plastic bag with the stems out. Secure the bag around the herb bunches, cutting holes in the sides of the bag to allow for air circulation. Hang the bunches by the stems and allow them to dry naturally. The bag will catch the herbs as they dry, crumble, and fall off of stems.

You can find air-drying racks for herbs at most garden centers, or online. The racks allow good airflow to dry the herbs over a few days or more. Place them near a window to allow sunlight to dry herbs. The air in your home should also be relatively dry.

Air Dry Outdoors

You need warm, dry air and sun to effectively dry herbs outdoors. You must also keep the herbs away from insects by using a fine screen that allows the sun to penetrate. Several types of drying racks work well outdoors.

You can also allow fennel, dill, coriander, mustard seed, and caraway to dry naturally on the vine in your potager garden. Do not harvest these herbs until they are completely dry and even the stems have shriveled. Do not harvest any moldy leaves or seeds.

You may want to complete the outdoor drying process indoors using the oven or a dehydrator to destroy any insect residue.

Freeze Dry

This is another way to preserve herbs. You can freeze herbs in plastic bags or containers. They will be limp when thawed, but are still good in stews, soups, and other dishes. Another method is to add water or a little olive oil to cut up or crushed herbs and freeze them in ice-cube trays.

Freezing herbs that dried outside or on the vine is also an excellent way to kill any invisible insect residue or other germs. Herbs dried outside should always be washed and dried first before freezing.

Saving Seeds from Your Garden

It may seem a given to simply order new seeds from the catalog each spring. In my grandparents' day, however, saving seeds was necessary if they hoped to grow a garden for the next year. Collecting and saving seeds from your garden is part of the gardening cycle and a skill in which many of today's gardeners are unfamiliar. Saving seeds can be another fun—and essential—aspect to potager gardening that aligns you more closely to the wheel of the year.

Reserving seeds from the harvest of your herbs, fruits, vegetables, and other plants not only saves money for the next planting season; seeds produced from your garden have the added benefit of being adapted to your location. Excess seeds can also be traded with other people. The satisfaction derived from preserving your own seeds only adds to the enjoyment of your potager garden.

Collecting and storing seeds correctly is essential for viability come planting time. Seeds from different flowers, herbs, vegetables, and fruits are collected and kept differently, and there are a multitude of online resources which provide information on saving seeds in great detail. To begin with, however, here are the basic seed-saving principles for various plants:

Flowers

It's time to harvest your flower seeds once the petals fall. Cut the flower head, remove the husks and foreign materials, and extract the seeds. Dry for around six to seven days. Store seeds in a labeled and sealed container/envelope in an excellent, dry location.

Herbs

To harvest seeds from your herbs, you must let the flowers develop. Let the plants mature, and when the heads or pods dry, you can harvest the seeds. Hold a basin below the heads and tip the pods to release the seeds. With some herbs, you may be required to crush or roll the heads between your hands. Once you have the seeds, let them dry for some time, and store them in an air-tight glass container in a dark and dry place at freezing temperatures. Remember to label the container.

Vegetables

For fruit-based vegetables, like tomatoes, wait until the fruits mature. Then cut the fruit open and extract the seeds. Allow the seeds to dry for several days. Place them in a sealed container. Store containers in a dry place at very low temperatures. For vegetables that produce pods, like kale, wait until the pods dry up. Cut off the pods and split them to get to the seeds. Let the seeds dry for several days. Place them in sealed glass containers and label.

Fruits

For wet fruits, you should select mature, ripe fruits to save the seeds. Split the fruits open to get the seeds. Dry the seeds for several days. For many large seed types, keep in sealed containers or a refrigerated room.

Where and How Can You Store Saved Seeds?

Once you place dried seeds in containers or sealed envelopes, a cool, dry, and dark location serves you best. You can store the seeds in a cold dark closet or a cool basement room. A refrigerated room is also suitable.

How Long Can Seeds Be Stored?

Seeds in good condition, dried and stored properly, can be kept for up to one year. However, depending on the plant, some seeds, like onion seeds, may last less than a year. Others, like lettuce, can be kept more than three years. Most annual flower seeds can be reserved for up to three years, while most vegetable seeds remain viable for one to two years. Most herb seeds in good condition can be stored for more than one year. Most fruit seeds will remain viable for at least one year.

Testing Germination in Older Seeds

The water test is the standard method of testing seed viability. Put some seeds in a basin of water. Allow them to rest for approximately 20 minutes. If the seeds sink, they can germinate. If they float, they have lost viability. You also test them using the "germination test" method. Place the seeds in damp cotton wool and fold. Put the folded wool in a zip-top plastic bag and seal it, then place the bag in a warm place. Viable seeds should germinate within several days to a few weeks.

Take the Potager Garden Challenge

As a beginner, it can be very intimidating to understand soils and seeds, becoming inundated by details. I had the benefit of absorbing knowledge from my parents and grandparents growing up, but I still had to just jump in and work through trial and error. I remember my first garden on my own. I was a bit overwhelmed with no one to oversee my work. I sat in the middle of the garden and said to my seeds, "I'm not completely sure that I know what I'm doing, so please don't die on me. Help me out." Best garden ever! I now realize my ancestors probably had to go through the same trials with their own gardens, adjusting when spring came late or the growing season was especially dry or rainy.

I believe that the first time you try anything always presents some difficulty, simply because there are so many questions you may have. Today, I recognize my grandpa in the way I pick up the soil and feel it. Like him, I work without a thermometer, soil samples, or formal measurements. I'm more comfortable doing "a handful of this" and "a handful of that."

You may be surprised to find that gardening by the school of hard knocks is more forgiving than you might think. I say to beginners: buy yourself a big pot, plant a bunch of herbs in it, and see what happens! Nothing compares to the feeling of triumph when they magically appear. Work with it and continue from there. Get in there and get yourself dirty! Instead of spending money on different landscapes that in the end just take up space, dig in that dirt, experience the joy of seeing the first seeds sprouting through the soil.

In taking the potager garden challenge, look at your own cooking…how many ingredients can you grow for yourself? Use this book to inspire yourself and remove your fear of gardening. Use it to try different types of foods to eat. Experiment and be creative. Potager gardening is about making your garden work for you.

When you start to connect to where your food comes from, I guarantee your experience with cuisine will completely change.

The rest of this book is filled with recipes that can be adapted to any diet with ingredients from any farmer's market. But it's my hope these recipes will inspire you to grow your own food, make up your own recipes, and enjoy the things you've grown in your own potager garden.

"Lettuce" begin!

Intro to Recipes

In this book, you'll find recipes containing ingredients that can mostly be grown in a potager garden. Vegetables, fruits, herbs, and edible flowers can come from your garden and be incorporated into the food you make. I want you to be inspired to plant the things you enjoy eating. Blend your fruits, vegetables, herbs, and flowers in creative dishes, desserts, and drinks.

Each of these recipes can be a stand-alone meal for just one person or scaled up for large groups. They can all adapt easily to gluten-free, dairy-free, or sugar-free diets. They can be kept vegetarian or vegan, or you can add a protein of your choice. Nothing is written in stone; you should feel confident incorporating various flavors and ingredients as needed.

Most importantly, there's no one right way to do anything in the kitchen. Take pride in the simple art of growing food in your garden—no matter its size—and cooking with those ingredients. Tap into your food memories, substitute what you like, and have fun.

Conversion Chart

Teaspoons	Tablespoons	Ounces	Cups	Pints	Quarts	Gallons	Milliliters	Liters
3	1	$^1/_2$	$^1/_{16}$				15	0.015
12	4	2	$^1/_4$				60	0.06
24	8	4	$^1/_2$				125	0.125
		16	2	$^1/_2$	$^1/_4$	$^1/_{16}$	250	0.25
		32	4	2	1	$^1/_4$	950	0.95
		128	16	8	4	1	3800	3.8

Key Volume Conversions

Use this quick cheat sheet for the equivalents:

1 tablespoon = 3 teaspoons = 15 milliliters
4 tablespoons = $^1/_4$ cup = 60 milliliters
1 ounce = 2 tablespoons = 30 milliliters
1 cup = 8 oz. = 250 milliliters
1 pint = 2 cups = 500 milliliters
1 quart = 4 cups = 950 milliliters
1 quart = 2 pints = 950 milliliters
1 gallon = 4 quarts = 3800 milliliters = 3.8 liters

Tip
3 parts fresh herbs to 1 part dried herbs (example: 3 tsp. fresh to 1 tsp. dried)

Oven Temperature Conversions

Fahrenheit	Celsius	Gas Mark	Terminology
275 degrees F	140 degrees C	1	Very Cool or Very Slow
300 degrees F	150 degrees C	2	Cool or Slow
325 degrees F	165 degrees C	3	Warm
350 degrees F	177 degrees C	4	Moderate
375 degrees F	190 degrees C	5	Moderate
400 degrees F	200 degrees C	6	Moderately Hot
425 degrees F	220 degrees C	7	Hot
450 degrees F	230 degrees C	8	Hot
475 degrees F	245 degrees C	9	Hot
500 degrees F	260 degrees C	10	Very Hot

Butternut Squash with Walnuts and Feta

As a vegetarian, I'm motivated by the idea that meat doesn't have to be the centerpiece of a holiday table. While turkey has its place, those of us who prefer a meatless meal shouldn't be resigned to a plateful of side dishes.

This recipe came about because I wanted a holiday-inspired main course that was something special to look at and slice into. You can make any variation by including ingredients you love, like cranberries, for a festive flair. It's a hearty and substantial main course and a lot more special than a plate of side dish vegetables.

We eat with our eyes first, and my presentation is always big, for lack of a better word. Instead of buying decorations, I love the creative aspect of using the food as décor on the table and the plate.

This hearty meal is perfect for a holiday dinner, a dinner party, or just because. You don't always need a reason to celebrate; we should celebrate every day with delicious food.

INGREDIENTS

1- 2½ lb. butternut squash, halved lengthwise

2 T olive oil, divided

½ C walnuts

1 C wild rice

1 small onion, chopped fine

2 cloves garlic, crushed

1 tsp. rosemary, finely chopped

⅛ tsp. ground cinnamon

1 C canned lentils, rinsed and drained

3½ oz. crumbled feta cheese

1 C baby spinach leaves, chopped

Tomato chutney *(see recipe in Accompaniments)*

INSTRUCTIONS

Preheat oven to 375 degrees F

Place squash halves cut side up, on a baking tray and brush with 1 tablespoon olive oil

Roast 1¼ hours or until tender

Set aside to cool

Arrange walnuts on the baking dish and roast for 3 to 5 minutes until toasted

Cool and chop coarsely

Cook wild rice per directions and drain

Heat remaining oil in a pan over medium heat

Add onion and garlic, sauté until softened

Stir in rosemary and cinnamon

Combine rice and the onion mixture in a large bowl

Add lentils, feta cheese, spinach, and walnuts and mix to combine

Add salt and pepper to taste

Use a spoon to scoop out the flesh of the squash, leaving about 1 inch inside the skin. You can use the scooped-out flesh in another recipe.

Divide the rice mixture in half and spoon it into each side of the squash, pressing it down firmly

Carefully place the halves together and tie 3 separate knots with string to hold together

Place on a baking tray and roast for 45 minutes or until tender

Transfer to a plate

Slice, adding a spring of rosemary (or any fresh herb sprig or edible flower) for garnish

Serve with tomato chutney

Cabbage and Vegetable Fritters
(with tomato and avocado salsa)

Cabbage fritters are a great casual appetizer, side dish, or standalone meal. I find these fritters particularly excellent as an accompaniment for breakfast. Use it as a replacement for hashbrowns with your eggs and go ahead and add a side of bacon or sausage if you like.

Don't forget, cabbage is a perfect choice for celebrating St. Patrick's Day. Serve these as a unique side with your corned beef. And pair it with a genuine pint of Guinness. Slainte!

INGREDIENTS

2 C napa cabbage, finely shredded

2 ears of corn, kernels removed

1 carrot, grated

1 small red pepper, diced

½ C Parmesan cheese, grated

⅓ C cheddar cheese, grated

½ C flour, sifted [add more if needed]

2 eggs

½ C buttermilk

Salt and pepper, to taste

Olive oil for frying

Options
Tomato & avocado salsa *(see recipe in Accompaniments)*
Crème fraiche or sour cream *(see recipe in Accompaniments)*
Serve with both as options for your guests

INSTRUCTIONS

Add cabbage, corn, carrots, red pepper, and cheese together in a large bowl and mix well

Stir in flour and mix

Whisk eggs, buttermilk, salt, and pepper together in a medium bowl

Add egg mixture to the vegetables and toss until combined

Heat a small amount of oil in a large frying pan over med heat

Spoon teaspoons onto the pan, cooking 3-4 minutes on each side (don't press the mixture down, or it will turn out paste-like)

Don't worry if it looks loose, the egg will hold it together

Transfer to a wire rack over a tray covered with a paper towel (or you can keep them warm in the oven while completing the following steps)

Sprinkle with chives

Serve them with tomato and avocado salsa, crème fraiche, or sour cream

Carrots with Lavender Honey

When you have control over your ingredients, you're more likely to engage with them and taste them in an entirely new way. Carrots are one of those ingredients because carrots, for me, are kind of funny: I placed them right above peas on the scale of things I didn't like as a child. And for some reason, I associated the way they were cut with how they tasted. I prefer cutting my carrots lengthwise like French fries rather than like coins. But since carrots are easy to grow, I put them in my garden and learned that the carrots you buy in the store aren't even close to tasting the same. Suddenly, I loved carrots.

I created this recipe during my "infused honey" phase. There was an apiary close by that sold local honey. I bought the honey and infused different herbs to give it a new flavor. Lavender, being so plentiful, was an obvious choice. Herbs are a big part of my food story. The smell of lavender brings me right back to my grandparents' home. I know lavender can be difficult for some people to get past. The idea that it's soap, not food, is a challenge. But I encourage you to think outside of the box and consider adding lavender to your food, both sweet and savory. And there's no better introductory recipe than carrots with lavender honey.

The orange in the recipe provides a touch of acidity to balance it all out. Pecan pieces add texture and protein.

INGREDIENTS

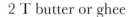

2 T butter or ghee

4 C carrots

⅓ C broth

1 tsp. orange zest

1½ tsp. parsley

¼ C lavender-infused honey *(see recipe in Accompaniments)*

Salt

Pecan pieces, for topping

INSTRUCTIONS

Melt butter in a large pan

Add carrots and sauté until almost tender

Add remaining ingredients

Simmer until carrots are soft and the liquid is thickened

Add salt to taste

Top with pecan pieces

Cauliflower Soup

I am just a peasant farmer at heart, but this recipe is exquisite enough for royalty!

Soup is always comfort food. We eat it when we don't feel well, when we're sad, or when we're cold. It's the kind of thing people bring to your home when you've had a loss. This cauliflower soup is hearty and creamy; it's a complete meal cooked in one pot. I drizzle olive or truffle oil on top, and add pepitas and crumbled bleu cheese when I present this.

I grew up on soup. Going to school in Chicago, I had to walk six blocks home for lunch and six blocks back in cold midwestern winters. I know it sounds like a cliché, but it's true: I had soup every day.

I usually only love cauliflower raw, but this soup is one of the few times I enjoy it cooked. If you don't usually like cauliflower, you may find your preferences changed after trying this soup. You will never be able to make enough for leftovers. This is a tasty, hearty soup with a lovely presentation.

INGREDIENTS

1 fresh cauliflower head, cut into florets

2 large white potatoes, peeled and chopped small

4 garlic cloves, chopped

1½ tsp. fennel seeds

¼ C olive oil + extra to drizzle on top to serve

1 large onion, chopped

2 tsp. thyme + extra to top

3 tsp. vegetable or chicken stock powder

1 ⅔ C water

1 ⅓ C light cream

⅓ C grated Parmesan cheese

⅓ C grated cheese

Salt and pepper to taste

Bleu cheese crumbles for topping

Pepitas for topping

Truffle oil to top (alternative option)

INSTRUCTIONS

Preheat oven to 400 degrees F

Place cauliflower, potatoes, garlic, and fennel seeds on a parchment-lined roasting pan

Drizzle approx. 2 T of olive oil onto mixture, toss to combine

Roast for 25 minutes or until tender

Reserve a few small cauliflower florets for topping later

Heat remaining oil in a saucepan on medium-high heat

Add onions and thyme and cook until softened

Add stock powder and 1 ⅔ C water, and bring to a simmer

Add roasted vegetables and cream, bring to a simmer again

Remove and let stand 5 minutes

Use an immersion blender for best results, or pour into a blender, blending until smooth

Return to medium-low heat and add cheeses until smooth

Add salt and pepper to taste

To serve, top each bowl of soup with a sprinkle of thyme and pepitas. Drizzle truffle oil or olive oil around it, and top with a few of the reserved cauliflower florets

Add bleu cheese crumbles to top

Tip
Cut cauliflower and potatoes the same small size so they bake evenly.

Cucumbers with Chives

This one is for my grandma. When I was growing up, cucumbers were just plain cucumbers for the most part. They might be sliced for salads, but most were pickled and preserved. But for special dinners or holidays, my grandmother always made this cucumber salad with sour cream and chives. That meant the event was fancy or celebratory. Instead of just slicing them up, she took the time to make something extraordinary out of the humble cucumber. If this dish was on the table, next to an assortment of olives and relishes, it was sure to set the stage for parties or holidays.

Constructing a cucumber salad like this makes something simple sing with love.

INGREDIENTS

2 cucumbers, cut into small cubes

1 clove of garlic, minced

¾ tsp. salt

1 small carton of sour cream *(see recipe for homemade sour cream in Accompaniments)*

2 T distilled red vinegar

¼ tsp. black pepper

Fresh chives, cut

INSTRUCTIONS

Mash garlic and salt together

Combine sour cream, salt and garlic mixture, vinegar, and pepper

Combine with cucumber and chill for at least 1 hour

Sprinkle with chives

Eggplant and Pepper Panini

Travel is an excellent way to expand your palate and try new things, and Europe is the epicenter for such discoveries. This recipe came from my deep, abiding love of ciabatta bread. I was hooked on it after traveling in Europe. There, cities have bakeries on every corner, and the smell of fresh bread is always in the air. Years ago, at a market in London, I had a turkey sandwich with mouthwatering orange cranberry ciabatta bread, and it changed my entire experience. It still amazes me today that you can make turkey sandwiches on different kinds of bread and create a whole new experience.

This sandwich recipe is also a great way to use the peppers in my garden. Since being a vegetarian for 25+ years, I decided to incorporate them into a hearty sandwich. I love eggplant, and the flavors work well together. And, of course, I could use up some of my basil.

It's so hearty and so flavorful that you don't have to be a vegetarian to enjoy it. The first time I made this, I ate it before remembering that I wanted to take a photo. It was that inviting!

INGREDIENTS

1 large eggplant, cut into 8 slices

2 large sweet peppers, sliced into large pieces

2 T olive oil

Salt to taste

4 ciabatta rolls, halved

8 slices of provolone cheese

Basil aioli sauce *(see recipe in Accompaniments)*

INSTRUCTIONS

Brush eggplant and sweet peppers with oil and season with salt

Grill approximately 3-4 inches away from the heat until tender

Chop peppers when cool

Spread both sides of ciabatta with 2 tbsp. basil aioli sauce *(see recipe in Accompaniments)*

On the top half, add cheese

On the lower half, add 2 slices of eggplant and pepper strips

Put ciabatta pieces together

Grill until cheese is melted with a panini press

Serve with additional basil aioli sauce on the side for dipping

A panini press is not necessary. You can use a pan on the stove and a spatula to flatten the sandwich. You can also use a waffle iron or a George Foreman®-type grill.

Fresh Garden Salsa

I'm not a fan of jarred salsa. I think all you ever taste is the spice level. It's too runny, and I prefer mine fresh and with texture. This recipe is a great way to use your tomatoes when they come in; I promise you'll have a lot for leftovers. Obviously, you can grab a bag of chips and dig in. Even using a lime-flavored chip changes the experience.

You can use salsa on anything, not just chips or tacos. I would put this on a breaded chicken cutlet with some spinach and feta cheese when I was eating meat. Use it on fresh fish tacos, a dollop on enchiladas, or with your burrito. Leftovers are fun on a cauliflower crust with goat or feta cheese for an appetizer, on pizza, or as a condiment for burgers. Heck, you can eat it as a salad or side dish with any meal. It's just that tasty! I once used it on plain white rice, making it unforgettable. Get creative!

INGREDIENTS

5 plum tomatoes, chopped small

7 red cherry tomatoes, chopped small

3 yellow cherry-sized tomatoes, chopped

3 orange cherry-sized tomatoes, chopped

1½ C mixed green, red, orange, and yellow peppers, chopped small

2 garden green onions, chopped

1 medium red or white onion, chopped small

1½ T fresh pineapple sage (optional, but terrific!)

½ tsp. cumin

¼ C parsley, finely chopped

2 T fresh cilantro, chopped small

1 T fresh chervil, chopped

3 T lime juice

2 T olive oil

1 tsp. salt

½ tsp. sugar

Jalapeno (optional for more kick)

Mix all ingredients together

Allow to set and chill for one hour

For more kick, add seeded and diced jalapeno

Tip
To keep tomatoes from juicing excessively, keep them separate until mixing together, then drain before serving.

Garden Coleslaw

Growing up in the Midwest, coleslaw was always at picnics or cookouts. In the South, it's practically a condiment, used on sandwiches and not just as a side dish. You can't forget to invite the coleslaw to a barbecue!

We rarely do coleslaw just for us, but I can admittedly make a meal out of this recipe. It's a perfect summertime side dish, and I love to use it when I make fish tacos, adding just a little extra spice or sriracha aioli sauce. This recipe is a little bit sweet and a little bit spicy. It's halfway between creamy and vinegary, so it's perfect for any palate.

INGREDIENTS

8 C cabbage, grated

1 carrot, shredded

3 T onion, grated

⅓ C sugar

½ tsp. salt

⅛ tsp. pepper

¼ C whole milk

¼ C buttermilk

2 T white vinegar

3 T lemon juice

½ C mayonnaise *(see recipe in Accompaniments)*

Optional: 1 T Dijon mustard

INSTRUCTIONS

Mix all ingredients together in a large bowl

Refrigerate 4-8 hours

To give it more kick, add the Dijon mustard

Garden Brunch Vegetable Scones

I love to host visitors, especially since moving to North Carolina from the Midwest; I have people stay with me from out of town all the time. I never wanted to use precious time cooking meals as visiting is more important to me.

Instead, I like to make this old family favorite: versatile garden vegetable scones that are perfect for a casual brunch with coffee or tea or to take on the go. They can also be cut in half and used for sandwiches. It makes a very filling meal. They're even great for a road trip. I like to make and freeze them to have on hand for myself.

It's breakfast, brunch, lunch, or a snack!

INGREDIENTS

1 T olive oil

½ C spring onions, sliced

2 ⅔ C bell peppers (red, yellow, and green) cut into small pieces

1½ C fresh spinach, stems removed

⅓ C shredded zucchini, drained

3 C all-purpose flour

1 T (level) baking powder

½ tsp. salt

½ tsp. coarse pepper

½ tsp. thyme

1 tsp. fresh basil, chopped

1 tsp. fresh rosemary

⅛ tsp. dried dill

½ tsp. sage

½ C cold, unsalted butter

3 oz. cold cream cheese, cut into ¼" cubes (about a ⅓ of an 8 oz. brick)

¾ C milk

1 egg, slightly beaten to brush on top

INSTRUCTIONS

Preheat oven to 400 degrees F

Line a baking tray with parchment paper for best results

Heat oil in a medium-sized skillet over medium-high heat

Add onions and bell peppers and sauté until softened

Add spinach to the skillet and cook until slightly wilted

Add zucchini for a minute

Set the skillet aside

Whisk dry ingredients together: flour, baking powder, salt and pepper, thyme, rosemary, basil, dill, and sage into a large bowl

Work the cold butter pieces into the flour mixture with your fingers, until pea-sized crumbs form

Work in cream cheese pieces

Gently mix in the cooked vegetables (evenly distribute the spinach through the dough)

Pour in ½ C of the milk and work into the flour mixture

Add remaining milk as needed; just enough to knead it

Knead dough about 4 times, incorporating it into a ball

Lightly flour a clean surface and gently place the ball on your surface

Pat and press into a disc that's about ¾" inch thick

Cut disc into 8 pie shaped wedges

Brush the top of the scones with the slightly beaten egg

Place the wedges on the baking sheet 1" apart

Bake about 20-25 minutes or until the middle is done

Dot scones with butter

While warm, sprinkle with dried basil, thyme, dill, sage, and a bit of coarse salt

Serve warm or room temperature with sliced tomatoes, bacon, or assorted cheeses

They will keep for several days if stored in an air-tight container.

Tip
For smaller scones, divide the dough into 2 halves and follow the same directions.

Kale Chips

Who doesn't like to snack on a bowl of potato chips when given the chance? But I know there are better alternatives, and you can grow them right in your garden. Kale chips are great as a side dish or just a snack. And it's fun to flavor them any way you like.

I'll be honest; I don't make them specifically to eat. I make them when I haven't gotten around to using my kale and it's about to go bad. When you're cooking for just a single person like me, you don't always get to everything in your refrigerator. Kale stays hearty for a long time, but when it goes bad, it happens fast. Before I let that happen, I make up a big batch of kale chips and put them in a mason jar…if they last that long.

If I'm short on veggies for the day, I'll grab some and snack; you can't eat just one. They're a perfect replacement for chips or popcorn when watching a movie.

Pro tip: spray olive oil using a mister so the kale isn't too wet when you bake it.

INGREDIENTS

1 bunch fresh kale, washed, spines removed, and completely dried for crispy chips

2-3 T olive oil

Salt

Optional: ¼ C Parmesan cheese, grated

INSTRUCTIONS

Wash and remove the spines, pat, and let dry

Toss kale with olive oil (or spray with the mister)

Lay kale on a parchment-papered baking sheet

Lightly salt

Sprinkle with Parmesan cheese

Bake approximately 5 to 6 minutes and turn

At around 10 to 12 minutes - they should be crisp

Remove from oven to cool

Variations can include adding lime juice and chili powder or your favorite spices

Lemon Parsnips and Carrots

This has to be one of my favorite recipes. Okay…I know I say that for all of my recipes, but this one has a special place for me. We all get burned out a little bit on carrots. Carrots are these poor little guys who look so sad on the plate with all the other food. I'm not a raw carrot person, but I do like them cooked with many other ingredients on them.

This recipe is made with dates that melt and become flavorful and naturally sweet. I've never met anyone who didn't like lemon parsnips and carrots when I served them. It's great as a side dish for a hearty fall meal.

INGREDIENTS

2 T olive oil

1 lb. fresh garden carrots, chopped into 1" pieces

1 lb. fresh parsnips, chopped into 1" pieces

6 cloves of fresh garlic

1 C water

3 tsp. chicken base

2 T fresh oregano, chopped

¾ C pitted dates, coarsely chopped

2 T seasoned butter *(see recipe in Accompaniments)*

2 T lemon juice (approximately 1 lemon)

INSTRUCTIONS

Preheat large pan

Add oil over medium heat

Add carrots, parsnips, and garlic

Cook, stirring occasionally, until lightly brown and beginning to soften

Add water, chicken base, oregano, dates, and herb butter

Cook until liquid is reduced (approx. 10 minutes)

Add lemon juice and serve

Parmesan Spaghetti Squash

Full of carbs and comfort, pasta is a favorite meal for so many people worldwide. But it isn't always the healthiest food. Using spaghetti squash in what would otherwise be a decadent carb-bomb is a great way to use more nutritious ingredients fresh from your garden.

The presentation is magnificent because you're serving the whole meal inside the squash. It's beautiful and tastes delicious. Everyone will eat an entire squash because it's just that good. It has everyone's favorite stuff, including cream and cheese, making it only a little healthier by using squash instead of pasta.

A lot of my squash recipes are a little bit more involved. Most squash varieties are harvested in the season most associated with big holiday meals. Like me, you still want something special if you don't eat meat. It's not poor me; I'm not short-changed. I love making entire courses out of these hearty autumn vegetables. You've dressed up this poor little squash in its Sunday best.

INGREDIENTS

1 medium spaghetti squash

1 tsp. olive oil

2½ T garlic, minced

5 oz. fresh spinach, chopped

½ C cream (heavy cream or half and half)

1 T cream cheese

Salt and pepper to taste

Grated or sliced mozzarella cheese, for topping

½ C Parmesan cheese (plus additional for topping)

Walnut pieces, to sprinkle on top

Optional: cooked bacon or ham pieces

INSTRUCTIONS

Preheat oven to 400 degrees F

Slice squash in half lengthwise, scoop out seeds

In a rimmed baking dish, place squash and rub olive oil on the cut side

Bake 40-45 minutes or until tender

While squash is roasting, start the sauce

In a medium pot, drizzle olive oil and heat over medium heat

Add garlic and sauté until fragrant

Add spinach and stir until gently wilted

Add cream, cream cheese, and Parmesan cheese, stirring well

Add salt and pepper to taste

Remove from heat

Once squash is done roasting, allow to cool

Separate the spaghetti squash into strands, leaving them in the shells

If using bacon or ham pieces, add them here

Pour the sauce over each squash boat

Stir to mix and top off with mozzarella cheese and additional Parmesan cheese

Bake at 350 degrees F for 20 minutes until bubbly

If not browned, place under broiler for one minute

Sprinkle with walnut pieces and serve

Peas with Mint and Lemon

When I was a kid, I would arrange my peas around the plate so no one noticed how many I'd avoided eating. Like most kids, I wasn't a fan. Sometimes I'd slip them under the rim of the plate so my parents and grandparents wouldn't see. You can imagine how well that worked once the table was cleared! My mother would call me by my first and middle name when, at last, she discovered the stash.

With time and flavor exploration, my palate matured, and I'm happy to announce that I eat my peas now. I don't just eat them, either—I love them. I prefer petite peas since I learned that I'm picky about the size of my vegetables, but that's the beauty of a potager garden. Grow whichever sized pea you want!

INGREDIENTS

½ C sweet red pepper, chopped

2 large onions, cut into wedges

2 T vegetable oil

16 oz. peas, cooked

2 T fresh mint, diced

¼ tsp. lemon zest, grated

INSTRUCTIONS

In a skillet, sauté red peppers and onions in oil until soft

Add peas and heat through

Add mint and lemon zest, cook one minute

Serve

Pesto

What do I do with my pile of basil? Make pesto, of course.

The applications for pesto are endless. You can freeze it in ice cube trays to keep individual serving sizes ready to go when you need them. Use it over your favorite pasta, in sandwiches, or as a stuffing. You can add your favorite flavors, like different cheeses or nuts, to make it your own.

At parties, I like to put out small bowls with various flavors of pesto—like a pesto bar—so everyone can have the flavor they want. Serve it with vegetables or crackers as a dip. It makes a great party dish with various presentations, and the bold green color looks impressive on your table.

INGREDIENTS

1½ C basil or herbs (parsley, spinach, etc.)

3 cloves garlic

½ C olive oil

½ C toasted pine nuts

½ tsp coarse salt

½-1 C Parmesan cheese

1 T lemon juice

INSTRUCTIONS

In a food processor, add basil and garlic, pulsing just enough to break up the garlic cloves

Drizzle in olive oil until you achieve a smooth green paste

Remove to a bowl

Toast pine nuts and allow to cool

Stir nuts, salt, Parmesan cheese, and lemon juice into the pesto

Additional Flavoring Suggestions – options are endless!

Spinach, basil, and jalapeno

Basil, sunflower seeds, and walnuts

Oregano

Potager Soup

I have never met a soup I didn't love. This particular recipe is a cross between what you would think of as a chicken noodle soup and a hearty vegetable soup. It's so colorful in your bowl that you'll have no trouble eating it. Trust me, though; it's worth it. I make it with orzo because it's a small pasta that cooks quickly. It's refreshing with a splash of lemon.

I grew up with soups, so I make a lot of them. They're year-round meals for me. This particular soup is by far the cleanest, most satisfying soup. For me, it would be a whole meal all by itself.

INGREDIENTS

½ C uncooked orzo pasta (cook separately for clear broth)

1 small onion, diced

3 carrots, diced

3 garlic cloves, finely chopped

6 C chicken or vegetable broth

½ C button mushrooms, sliced and slightly browned in butter

2 T fresh dill, chopped to garnish

2 T lemon juice

1½ C fresh baby spinach, stems removed

½ tsp. parsley

4-6 fresh mint leaves, chopped fine

Salt and pepper, to taste

Optional: 1 sprig of lemon thyme

Optional: 2 C cooked chicken, diced

INSTRUCTIONS

Make orzo pasta according to the directions

In a large pot cook onions, carrots, and garlic with the broth until tender

Add cooked orzo pasta to broth mixture, simmer uncovered for 5 minutes

Stir in mushrooms, dill, and lemon juice

Turn off the heat, add spinach and let it wilt without cooking it

Add parsley and mint when ready to serve

Optional: for a heartier soup, add 2 C diced chicken

Tip
When making ahead, omit spinach and orzo until reheated halves and follow the same directions.

Potato Soup

Potato soup is one of the first things I learned to make by myself as a young girl. Potatoes are among the most accessible ingredients for beginners. I could make this dish by myself when I was only ten or twelve without having to stand over a hot stove for hours on end. As I got older, I added my own flair to this simple dish to make it more impressive and delicious. For me, it's all about the toppings.

My father was the one who watched over my shoulder when I first made this one. He liked potato soup, too…and later, especially mine!

INGREDIENTS

5 potatoes, peeled, diced, and cubed

1 medium onion, finely diced

2 small garden carrots, diced

3¾ C chicken broth

Salt and white pepper, to taste

⅓ C butter

⅓ C flour

1½ C milk or cream (I mix both together)

½ C crème fraiche or sour cream *(see recipes in Accompaniments)*

Splash of buttermilk

Chives

Grated cheese, Parmesan or cheddar, or gouda (or a combination!)

Optional: bacon or ham for a heartier soup

INSTRUCTIONS

Add diced potatoes, onions, carrots, and chicken broth to a soup pot

Season with salt and pepper to taste

Cook over medium-high heat until it boils

Reduce heat and cook until tender

Make roux:

In another pot, melt butter over medium heat

Add flour and whisk constantly

Slowly add milk, whisking until thickened

Combine softened potatoes, carrots, and onion with broth and flour mixture

(you can use an immersion blender until the soup is smooth)

Add splash of buttermilk

Stir in the crème fraiche or sour cream and mix well

Fill each bowl

To serve, add toppings in the middle of the bowl: chives, cheese, bacon, or other toppings you enjoy

Quinoa with Raisins

Here's a recipe to challenge your idea of what a savory meal can be. I use rosewater in this one, which you can find in the Accompaniments section of this book. Rosewater is used in savory dishes across the Mediterranean and Middle East.

Ancient grains are trendy right now. When I was younger, I never even heard the word "quinoa"; I'm sure I couldn't have spelled it if you asked me to. Now I consider it a staple that's always on hand. You can use plain quinoa, but I like to use the tricolor variety. It's pretty and contains different nutrients. You can also make this recipe with couscous, pearled barley, or farro. I know that when you buy a container of these grains, you only use a cup at a time and realize a month later that you have all these grains on your shelves. Recipes like this are fantastic to have in mind for using up those grains.

Tip
This is eaten cold or at room temperature, which makes it a great choice for get-togethers.

Pro Tip
I like to keep quinoa vacuum-sealed in a jar to keep it fresh.

INGREDIENTS

1 C uncooked quinoa, rinsed

2 C water

¼ tsp. salt

½ C raisins

2 garlic cloves, minced

1 small onion, chopped fine

½ C parsley, chopped

½ green pepper, finely chopped

½ red pepper, finely chopped

Quinoa Dressing

2½ tsp. rosewater *(see recipe in Accompaniments)*

4 T lemon juice

¼ C + 1 T olive oil

½ tsp. salt and pepper, to taste

Mix and refrigerate

INSTRUCTIONS

Add uncooked quinoa to a saucepan, add water and salt

Bring to a boil, then reduce heat and cook until water is absorbed

Remove from heat, cover, and set aside

Let set for 5 minutes, then fluff up the quinoa in a bowl

Add raisins, garlic, onion, parsley, and peppers to a second bowl

Make dressing and add to raisins/vegetables, mixing thoroughly

Add fluffed quinoa to the vegetable/dressing mixture

Cover and refrigerate for 1 hour

Optional: add walnut pieces for additional protein

Rainbow Swiss Chard

Most of the recipes in this book have a lot of ingredients in them…except this one. A potager garden is stunning with these lovely leafy veggies. They're colorful, healthy, and not the most common to plant or eat; but I would love to change that. I encourage you to try and grow these colorful gems!

Swiss chard can be used on pizza, with fish dishes, soups, salads, and just about anything that you might make with spinach.

INGREDIENTS

Olive oil

1 bunch rainbow Swiss chard, stems snipped off

2 garlic cloves, sliced

Parmesan cheese, grated

Lemon juice, sprinkle

Salt to taste

Optional: additions include pine nuts, walnuts, and pecans

INSTRUCTIONS

Add oil to a pan on medium heat so the garlic doesn't burn

Add garlic and the Swiss chard

Cook 7-10 minutes until tender, tossing

Sprinkle in a handful of Parmesan cheese

Drizzle in a few drops of lemon juice

Red Lentil Penne Salad

Pasta and cheese—you can't go wrong. I make pasta for dinner all the time and am always thinking two steps ahead, wondering what else I can make. Sometimes simply adding cheese and putting it back in the oven is enough to transform a pasta recipe. I like cooking with a variety of pastas and am amazed how the same sauce can taste completely different with different pasta shapes!

This recipe is versatile in that you can take any type of penne and make a salad out of it. Red lentil pasta has more nutrients than classic penne. It's chewier than traditional pasta when it's cooked, so choose regular penne if you don't like al dente. I encourage you to get out of your comfort zone and try a pasta you've never used before. Experiment to find what you like or use what you have based on your budget.

I'm a one-pot dinner kind of gal. Cooking everything in the same pot makes cleaning afterward so much easier, especially when life gets busy. I might dress this recipe up a little more for company, but typically I'll just put it in a bowl and it's perfect. I've always thought that spinach tortellini sounded delicious with this recipe, and you can always use the pesto recipe (from earlier) on any leftover tortellini.

INGREDIENTS

2 C butternut squash, peeled, de-seeded, and cut into 1" pieces

Salt to taste

1 T olive oil

¼ tsp. cumin seeds, crushed

¼ tsp dried chili flakes

2 C kale leaves

1 box red lentil penne (or plain—red lentil penne can be a bit chewy)

¼ C walnuts, toasted

½ C spinach

Feta cheese crumbles

Tahini dressing (recipe below)

Tahini Dressing

⅓ C tahini

2½ T olive oil

2 T lemon juice, fresh

4 tsp. apple cider vinegar

2 garlic cloves, crushed

¼ C warm water

¼ C coriander leaves, finely chopped

Combine tahini, oil, lemon juice, vinegar, and garlic in a small container or jar

Stir in water until the mixture loosens

Add coriander, season, and stir until combined

INSTRUCTIONS

Preheat oven to 400 degrees F

Line 2 baking trays with parchment paper

On tray #1, place squash, seasoned with salt and a drizzle of oil

Bake 25 minutes until golden

Sprinkle with cumin and chili flakes

On tray #2, place kale and spray with oil

Return squash to oven along with kale and bake until kale is crispy, approximately 10 minutes

Cook pasta in a large saucepan per the directions on the box

Add 1 tbsp. cooking liquid to the tahini dressing (below), stir and combine

Drain pasta and transfer to a bowl

Toss ¾ of the tahini dressing through the pasta

Serve pasta topped with squash, kale, and remaining dressing

Add walnuts and feta cheese over dish

Refrigerator Bread and Butter Pickles

I don't eat as many sandwiches as I did in the old days but boy! I love to eat the bread and butter pickles that go in them, even by themselves. I just make them in a gallon jar and try not to eat too many. They're sweet, but not as sweet as store-bought pickles, and will go with anything you're making.

Occasionally I eat pre-made vegan burgers, but they don't have a lot of "get-up-and-go" straight out of the package and require some dressing up. These pickles are a great addition. Pickles make a great little side dish, going along with whatever protein I eat in the day. I always have them as a relish on the table. And who doesn't love homemade pickles? When you put them on the table, and everyone comments on how good they are, you can proudly say, "I made them!"

INGREDIENTS

2 C distilled vinegar

1 C apple cider vinegar

2 C sugar

½ C brown sugar

2-3 tsp. mustard seeds

1 tsp. celery seed

½-1 tsp. turmeric

10 C cucumbers, skin on, washed and sliced

2½ T kosher salt

2 sweet onions, sliced

Vinegar Brine

In a medium pot, add both vinegars, sugar, and brown sugar

Mix together on low heat until the mixture boils, stirring constantly

Add the mustard seed, celery seed, and turmeric

Return it to a boil and let it cool down completely

Tip
This brine is good for pickling many things, including green tomatoes, okra, or squash. When your cucumber patch comes in quickly, this is a lovely way to add to summer dishes without a canning process.

INSTRUCTIONS

Spread half the cucumbers in a large bowl

Add some of the salt and layer again

Place bowl in the refrigerator, covered, from 2-24 hours to crisp things up!

Rinse the salt from the pickles

Add onions and mix into the cucumbers

Put pickle-and-onion mixture into a gallon jar

Add the brine, pushing the pickles down until fully immersed

Let set in the refrigerator for 1 week

Enjoy!

Refrigerator Yellow Squash Pickles

When your garden is exploding squash, this recipe is a saving grace. Yellow squash comes into the garden fast and furious, and can only be fried up with zucchini, onions, and tomatoes so many times. These pickles are so easy, featuring a brine that is just different enough, and oh-so-delicious. It's not just a pickle; with bigger pieces of peppers, it transforms into a side dish. The squash is colorful and looks gorgeous on tablescapes all year long.

INGREDIENTS

6 small yellow summer squash, sliced thin (zucchini can also be used, or mix them!)

2 large sweet red peppers, cut into ¼" strips

2 red onions, sliced

1 sweet onion, sliced

1½ T salt

2 C sugar

1½ C white vinegar

1½ tsp. mustard seed

1½ tsp. celery seed

1 tsp. dill weed

½ tsp. ground mustard

Optional: 3 sprigs of lemon thyme

INSTRUCTIONS

Put sliced squash, red peppers, and onion into a colander with a plate underneath

Add salt and toss, letting juices drain for one hour

Lightly pat with a clean flour sack towel to remove any excess salt

In a saucepan, combine remaining ingredients and bring to a boil, stirring to dissolve sugar

Let cool

Add vegetables to a 2-quart mason jar (add optional lemon thyme at this point)

Add cooled-down brine and pour into the jar, covering vegetables

Push the vegetables down, making sure that they're completely covered in brine

Refrigerate 4 days before serving

Store for up to 3 weeks in the refrigerator

Rosemary Green Beans

The intent of this book is to give you customizable recipes to make, especially for things grown in your garden (otherwise, it's all the same!). Remember that we eat with our eyes too, so adding colorful herbs and dressing the plate will contribute to everyone's enjoyment. I'm all about setting a colorful table.

Green beans go with anything and everything. They're prolific to cuisines, here and overseas, so you need a lot of green bean recipes in your toolbox. Frankly, you can never add too many things to beans; the basic idea here being versatility. You can further personalize this by adding other ingredients that you love, like mushrooms. During the holidays, throw cranberries in this dish to add a festive flair.

I love green beans long rather than cut up. For some reason, they taste better to me that way. They're also easier to cook; you don't have the work of cutting them up.

INGREDIENTS

1 lb. green beans, cleaned and trimmed but left long

4 T butter

1 fresh sprig of rosemary leaves

1 T lemon juice

3 garlic cloves, minced

1 tsp. fresh thyme

½ C pecans

INSTRUCTIONS

Steam green beans for about 10 minutes

In a saucepan mix butter, rosemary, lemon juice, garlic, thyme, salt, and pepper

Pour lemon dressing over green beans and add pecans

Optional: add nutmeg, fried mushrooms, and/or cranberries for a more festive holiday dish

Stuffed Squash Blossoms

One of my favorite aspects of potager gardening is getting to use the entirety of the plant while cooking. I can't help but to applaud my own resourcefulness when I use every part of the plant to make something incredible. You can use the roots, flowers, or leaves for different purposes. This recipe helps channel the resourceful gardener in all of us by putting the blossoms of your zucchini and squash to delicious use. You can use any squash blossoms, but zucchini squash is the biggest, therefore the most straightforward for use in this recipe.

When I was younger, my grandfather would show up with armfuls of giant zucchinis; I struggled to find so many uses for them. If I had known about this recipe then, I would have picked all the blossoms before they took fruit, then he wouldn't have had so many to pawn off on me!

If you love zucchini, you'll want to plant extra to get enough blossoms to make this recipe. It's a real show stopper. It seems complicated, but it isn't as hard as it sounds. I don't typically make it just for myself because I would eat all of them, but guests will think you're a Michelin Star chef if you make this.

Remember: you can't save squash blossoms.

INGREDIENTS

Cheese Filling

18 zucchini blossoms, stamens removed

3 oz. goat cheese

3 oz. cream cheese

1/2 tsp. red pepper flakes

1/2 tsp. dried oregano

1/4 tsp. dried basil

1 clove garlic

Salt and pepper to taste

Blossom Preparation

Swish blossoms in cold water and drain on a paper towel

Pat dry and set aside

Mix goat cheese, cream cheese, red pepper flakes, oregano, basil, garlic, salt, and pepper until blended

Gently fill each blossom with about 2 tsp. cheese filling (a pastry bag or small spoon works well)

Refrigerate while making the batter

Beer Batter

$\frac{1}{8}$ C cornstarch

$\frac{1}{2}$ C flour

$\frac{1}{2}$ tsp. salt

$\frac{1}{4}$ tsp. pepper

$\frac{1}{4}$ tsp. celery salt

$\frac{1}{4}$ tsp. baking soda

$\frac{1}{2}$ tsp. baking powder

1 egg, beaten

$\frac{1}{2}$ C cold, flat beer

For Frying

Vegetable oil (enough for 2 inches in your skillet)

Salt and pepper, to taste

Grated Parmesan cheese

Chopped chives

INSTRUCTIONS

Heat skillet with 2 inches of oil to 375 degrees F

While oil is heating, whisk together beer batter ingredients until combined

Carefully dip a stuffed blossom into the batter, covering the entire flower

Ease into the hot oil, browning on one side before turning and browning the second side

Using a slotted spoon, remove blossom and place on a paper towel to drain

Make sure they don't touch! And don't make too many at once

Sprinkle each blossom with salt and pepper; garnish with Parmesan cheese and

chopped chives

Sweet Potato Couscous Salad

I'll admit it: I struggle to make perfect rice. I can cook anything you ask, so long as it's not rice; it often clumps when I try to cook it. I've been known to run to a Chinese restaurant to get takeout rice after ruining a batch. Rather than go through all that hassle, I find couscous or other ancient grains much easier (while having more nutrients). Of course, I now have a rice cooker but still enjoy the flavorful taste of grains.

You can use any grain with this recipe and it will be delicious. For those who don't like romaine, substitute spinach or kale. It's meant to be served at room temperature, but I will eat it right out of the fridge. I add nuts to give it protein and make it a meal.

INGREDIENTS

3½ C sweet potatoes, peeled and cut into wedges

2 T olive oil

1 C pearl couscous

1 15-oz. can black beans, drained and rinsed

4 green onions, thinly sliced

2 T fresh dill, chopped

¼ C roasted almonds, chopped

1 T balsamic vinegar

2 baby romaine leaves, trimmed

⅓ C goat or feta cheese, crumbled

¼ C pomegranate arils

Several drops lemon juice

INSTRUCTIONS

Preheat oven to 425 degrees F

Line a baking tray with parchment and add sweet potatoes

Drizzle with 1 T oil

Bake until tender

Make couscous per directions

When done add black beans, green onions, dill, almonds, roasted sweet potatoes, balsamic vinegar, and remaining oil in a large bowl

Salt and toss

Divide romaine lettuce in shallow bowls and top with sweet potato mixture

Sprinkle with goat or feta cheese, pomegranate arils, and drops of lemon juice

Chill or serve at room temperature

Zucchini Eggplant Strudel

I appreciate the artful aspect of food. Presenting a beautiful dish shows your family or guests that you took the time to make something special. I often add edible flowers or herbs to my dishes so they look like a renaissance painting. This delicious dish also boasts a beautiful presentation.

You can choose any veggies from your garden, as well as any cheeses. Use the same vegetables that you'd use for an everyday dish, just dressed up. You will also use phyllo dough, which you can find in the frozen food aisle of your supermarket. (I don't make my dough, and believe it or not, most Greek yia-yias don't make their phyllo dough either.)

INGREDIENTS

Enough frozen phyllo dough for 6 layers of 14 x 8 sheets

2 zucchinis, cut into bite-sized pieces

1 large eggplant

1 large red pepper, chopped

1 small onion, chopped

½ bag frozen artichoke hearts

Olive oil

3 garlic cloves

Salt to taste

Black pepper

Garlic granules

Italian seasoning

Romano cheese, fresh

Mozzarella cheese, fresh

Grated fontina cheese

Asiago cheese

Grated cheese for topping

Marinara sauce (for dipping)

INSTRUCTIONS

Defrost phyllo dough

Roast vegetables ahead of time, dicing them and drizzling with olive oil, salt, pepper, garlic granules, and Italian seasoning to taste

Bake at 425 degrees F until tender

For each of the 6 sheets of dough: spray with olive oil and sprinkle grated Romano cheese, keeping the dough covered with a damp cloth as you work with each layer

Upon reaching the 6th layer, spread your vegetables over it, leaving a 2-inch border all the way around

Sprinkle asiago cheese, mozzarella cheese, and fontina cheese over vegetables

Fold the edge ends over the vegetables and carefully roll up, starting on the longer side until it becomes a log

Spray olive oil on the top of the log along with grated cheese and coarsely ground black pepper

Bake for about 20 minutes at 400 degrees F until golden

Let it cool down before you slice and dip in marinara sauce

Intro to Desserts

Nothing is more exciting after an amazing meal than a plate of beautiful, homemade desserts. I enjoy sharing desserts with friends and family, just like my grandmother did. I've included just a sample of delicious desserts that can be made with many ingredients from your garden, including herbs and edible flowers.

My grandmother was the baker of all bakers. Walking into the kitchen was like walking into a professional bakery, even though she worked without all the fancy mixers or gadgets. It was incredible what she could do with just a mixing bowl and an egg beater. And she didn't just make one cake at a time; she would have a dozen desserts lining the table. Grandma prided herself in creating amazing things using only the ingredients she had on hand.

While baking does require a bit more precision than other types of cooking, I also believe that desserts should be accessible. So, I've created simple recipes to incorporate your own favorite flavors.

I also feel that cakes should have natural ingredients. The best decoration on a baked item is an edible flower or herb. It's a way to go that extra mile, just like Grandma did. No matter how long I bake or how much I try, I will always strive to live up to Grandma's ability in the kitchen.

Don't forget, food is communal, so make enough to share with friends and family.

17th Century Sugared Violets

Do you remember store-bought cakes that had those hard little sugar confections? They would taste like sugar cubes cut into a flower, and we fought over them as children. This is a much more refined version.

I'm not quite from the seventeenth century, but I love this sweet, historic recipe, no pun intended. I often wonder if this was the task older women gave to children to keep them out of the way in the kitchen. Kids would do every part, from gathering the perfect violets to the sugaring. It's so straightforward anyone can do it.

These are great on any pastry for added delight.

If you're resourceful and artsy, this one is for you. You can use a few different kinds of flowers for this. Tiny flowers are fun because you can decorate them creatively. Create food fit to inspire with these lovely, sugared violets.

INGREDIENTS

2 egg whites

Castor sugar

4 oz. violets (pesticide free), stems attached

INSTRUCTIONS

Gently clean and rinse violets one by one, or spray and dry on a paper towel

Slightly whisk the egg white

Use a small brush or new paintbrush to paint egg white all around each flower

Lay on parchment paper and remove stems

Sprinkle with castor sugar and let dry for a few days in a cool, dark place

When completely dried, store in a covered container or jar

Afternoon Tea Puffs

Tea Puffs: the lovely combination of a cream puff and a scone. This delectable treat is the best food combination since peanut butter and jelly. They're great with tea and coffee (I make my own teas, or I'll brew up some flavored coffees for friends).

Everyone has their morning rituals, and these are certainly a big part of my own. I bake batches at a time, and they're always eaten until the plate is empty. I switch things up by making some with morning ingredients, like cinnamon, and others filled with custard for a sweet treat in the afternoon. You can make a lot of different things with the same base recipe, and you can use any flavor you want. Custard or jam is excellent. Or fill with tomato and basil for a savory treat. Use what you have and get creative.

PS: they're also great with wine!

INGREDIENTS

1½ C all-purpose flour

1½ tsp. baking powder

½ tsp. salt

¼ tsp. nutmeg

½ C sugar

⅓ C shortening

1 egg, room temperature

½ C milk, room temperature

Icing-Lemon Glaze

1 C powdered sugar

2 tsp. lemon zest

2 T lemon juice

1 T milk

Alternate Glaze

2 T butter, melted

2 T juice from crushed strawberries

½ tsp. almond extract

½ tsp. vanilla extract

1½ C powdered sugar

Tip
Add sugar one quarter tsp. at a time until glaze reaches the right consistency.

Preheat oven to 350 degrees F

Grease muffin tin or line with parchment paper

Whisk together flour, baking powder, salt, nutmeg, and sugar

Slightly whisk egg and add to shortening

Stir dry mixture into shortening mix, alternating with portions of the milk

Mix, but don't overwork the dough

Spoon each muffin tin until ⅔full

Bake for 20 to 30 minutes and remove from oven

While the puffs are cooling but still a bit warm, liberally drizzle with icing and add a small edible flower on top before it sets

Options

Add fresh whipping cream to the tea puffs with blueberries and strawberries on top, along with candied violets, edible flowers (such as forget-me-nots), or fruit blossoms (such as strawberry, raspberry, apple, pear, or cherry)

For a morning choice, dip them in warm, melted butter and cover in cinnamon sugar.

Peach Mint Sherbet

I use blackberry, raspberry, and strawberry bushes as borders in my potager garden. Others plant fruit trees like cherry, plum, or fig. I love to use these fruits in dishes you might not expect so they add an exciting layer of flavor, such as in meat dishes or gravy.

But ice cream is my weakness. Wherever I live, I always seem to end up living near an ice cream factory…dangerous for the pocketbook and the waistline! I started making my own ice cream, and quickly discovered how easy it was!

Sherbet is one of my favorite after-dinner desserts because it's so refreshing. I make this sherbet with peaches because peach trees are accessible to me, but you can make it with whatever fruit is available: lemon, lime, strawberry—even fruit that your neighbor graciously shares with you.

This is a super simple recipe. Anyone can make it, including children, so get them involved.

Tip
This is creamiest when eaten right away.

INGREDIENTS

6-8 ripe peaches, sliced and peeled

½ -1 C sugar or honey

2 T orange or lemon juice

2 mint leaves, finely chopped

¼ C heavy cream

INSTRUCTIONS

Spread peaches on an open tray and set in the freezer for one hour uncovered

Add frozen peaches, sugar, juice, and mint to a blender

Add heavy cream and blend

Put in container and freeze

Rose Petal and Vanilla Cookies

My Favorite Flower
My favorite flower is a rose growing in my yard.
I hold the stem, and with my nose, I sniff it very hard.
It pleases me to have this smell in my hand right here.
Where for a while I can tell, my favorite thing is near.

—by Katie, 5th Grade

These cookies mean a great deal to me because my birthday is on Valentine's Day. Like any other holiday baby, you don't want to make the day all about yourself when getting together with other people. I make these as a special Valentine's Day treat to share with friends, using a heart-shaped cookie cutter for the added visual.

Growing roses is in my blood—my grandmother had a rose nursery and was a rose expert. And I love working with rose petals; you can do so much with them and they have such a beautiful flavor. Different kinds of roses will vary in color and taste. They're beautiful in teas, great for making rosewater, and stunning as cake decorations. It seems a waste only to tend them in a garden.

INGREDIENTS

2¼ C flour

¼ tsp. salt

1 C unsalted butter

⅔ C powdered sugar

2 tsp. lemon zest

3¾ tsp. rosewater *(see recipe in Accompaniments)*

¼ tsp. vanilla extract

2 tsp. dried (pesticide-free) rose petals, crushed and finely chopped

3 tsp. milk

1 egg yolk

Sift flour and salt together and set aside

Cream butter and sugar using a mixer on medium for 3 minutes

Add lemon zest, rosewater, vanilla, crushed rose petals, milk, and egg yolk

With mixer on low, slowly add the dry ingredient mixture until incorporated

Once the dough is mixed, divide in half on parchment paper lightly dusted with flour

Roll out both halves separately into ¼" thick circles

Place both circles on baking sheets, cover with plastic wrap, and chill for two hours in the refrigerator

Once chilled, lift parchment paper off the tray to your workspace

Work with one chilled tray at a time

Run a long knife or utensil under the dough if it sticks

Use a cookie cutter to cut out cookies

Place cookies back on baking sheet lined with parchment paper

Cover tray with plastic wrap and chill 20 minutes

Bake at 350 degrees F for 10 to 12 minutes

Transfer to a baking rack to cool completely

Chocolate Topping

4 oz. white or dark chocolate

1 lemon, for zesting

Dried (pesticide-free) rose petals

Place white or dark chocolate in a microwave-safe bowl

Set heat to 50% on microwave and heat in 30-second intervals, stirring until smooth

Do not overcook—otherwise chocolate will get hard

Use a spoon to drizzle chocolate on cookies or dip half of each cookie into chocolate (it's lovely to plate using both methods)

Place on a cooling rack and immediately dust with zested lemon and garnish with rose petals

Allow half an hour to set before serving

Rosewater Lavender Cookies

Some people don't like the taste of lavender because it reminds them of their soap. A few decades ago, I was one of those people. It tasted like bug spray to me. But my palate changed when I got into aromatherapy and essential oils. I grew fond of the scent of lavender, and I love it now in food as well.

I make these cookies alongside the rose petal and vanilla cookies. They look so gorgeous on the plate with the purple and pink decorations that I like to think of them as companion cookies. One or two batches are never enough!

INGREDIENTS

½ C butter, softened

1 C granulated sugar

2 eggs

1½ C flour

1 tsp. lavender buds, crushed and pesticide free

2 tsp. baking powder

¼ tsp. salt

2 C powdered sugar

5½ tsp. water

6½ tsp. rosewater *(see recipe in Accompaniments)*

INSTRUCTIONS

Preheat oven to 375 degrees F

Cream butter and sugar

Add eggs, flour, lavender, baking powder, and salt, blending well

Drop by teaspoons onto a parchment-lined baking tray

Bake 8 to 10 minutes

Icing

Mix powdered sugar with water and rosewater

Drizzle over cookies after they've cooled and add a sprinkle of lavender buds

Zucchini Bread

I'm programmed for seasonal eating and always get excited for the season ahead and the dishes that come with it. When I see zucchini, I know summertime is almost over. You know the holidays are coming, so you're freezing foods and doing all the things to get ready. I have a persistent memory of my grandfather pawning off his zucchinis, and me not knowing what to do with them. I had to figure it out fast!

This recipe signals "end of summer, here comes fall" for me. Everyone should have a version of zucchini bread in their recipe files. It's a classic for a reason. But I don't love all the recipes out there; many are too dry.

The magic in this recipe that keeps it moist is the pineapple. I used pineapple in many things like Jell-O molds and pineapple upside-down cakes. Growing up, we used it in our house to replace sugar. It was an ah-ha moment that led me to add it to the zucchini bread.

Tip
You can grate zucchini and freeze it. I put it in one-cup packages so it's easy to portion. You can pull it out and use it as needed. Now I never have a surplus of zucchini bread.

INGREDIENTS

Butter for coating loaf pans

2-3 C zucchini, grated and drained

3 C all-purpose flour

1 tsp. baking soda

1 tsp. baking powder

1 tsp. salt

3 tsp. cinnamon

¾ tsp. nutmeg

3 eggs

2 C sugar

1 C vegetable oil

2 tsp. vanilla

½ carrot, grated

8 oz. canned pineapple tidbits, drained

1 C walnuts, chopped

1 C golden raisins

INSTRUCTIONS

Butter two 5x9 loaf pans

Drain zucchini in a colander

In a medium bowl, whisk flour, baking soda, baking powder, salt, cinnamon, and nutmeg

Beat eggs with a mixer for 1 minute

Add sugar and beat 1 minute

Add oil and vanilla, beat until thick

Stir in zucchini, carrots, pineapple, walnuts, and raisins

Fill loaf pans and bake at 350 degrees F for 55 minutes

Accompaniments

Basil Aioli

¾ C mayonnaise (see recipe on the next page)

⅓ C fresh basil, chopped

3 T Parmesan cheese, grated

2 T fresh chives, minced

1 T lemon juice

2 garlic cloves

½ tsp. salt

½ tsp. pepper

Instructions

Place all ingredients in a blender, cover and process until smooth

Crème Fraiche

2 C heavy cream

2 T cultured buttermilk

Instructions

Mix ingredients, cover, and set on counter to culture 12 hours

Refrigerate up to two weeks

Lavender Honey

1 pint-size canning jar, sterilized

1 C lavender buds, pesticide free

1 C honey

Instructions

Fill the pint jar with lavender

Pour honey over herbs

Add water to a pan, place the jar in the water, and heat on low to release the essential oil – don't boil!

Remove from heat, cover, and let sit for at least a week

Strain for a clearer honey and pour into a clean jar

Optional flavors: chamomile, rose petal, mint, lemon verbena, and rosemary

*Honey is a natural preservative and has a long shelf life

Mayonnaise

1 egg yolk

1 pint Mazola® corn oil

3 T tarragon vinegar (don't substitute—it won't have the taste that you hoped for!)

1-2 slivers of garlic, crushed

½ tsp. salt

Instructions

Beat yolk gradually, adding oil a little at a time until used up

Add vinegar and the rest of the ingredients

Rosewater Recipe

Roses and I go back a long way. It makes me happy to use this flower's extra layer of flavor as often as possible when I cook, so I like to make rosewater and keep it on hand. You can even freeze it to use later. There are so many uses, and not just for baking: it's great with vegetables, with rice, or in brown gravy. Things without much flavor on their own can be amped up with a bit of rosewater.

Ingredients

2 C fresh rose petals or 1 C dried petals, pesticide free

2 C distilled water

Instructions

Add rose petals to a small pot along with the distilled water

Stir until the petals are completely covered

Heat pot on low, stir, and cover for 20 minutes

Strain through a cheesecloth

Cover until cooled at room temperature

Pour into a covered jar and refrigerate

Seasoned Herb Butter

½ C unsalted butter

1 tsp. lemon juice

2-3 T fresh herbs, chopped fine

Instructions

Soften butter, add remaining ingredients

Cream together well

Note: If you have small silicon molds, you can make individual shapes

Sour Cream

1 C buttermilk or cream

1 tsp. distilled white vinegar (or lemon juice)

¼ C whole milk

Instructions

Add ingredients to a sterilized jar, cover with lid

Put in a warm place for 12-24 hours

Ready when thick and creamy

Refrigerate up to 2 weeks

Tomato Avocado Salsa

2 tomatoes, finely chopped

½ red onion, finely chopped

½ lime, grated and juiced

1 avocado, finely chopped

Instructions

Mix all ingredients together and refrigerate

Tomato Chutney

Tomatoes are prolific. Regardless of what variety you grow, you'll have more than you know what to do with, and you can only give so many to your neighbors. Even making salsa can get old fast. To create a different flavor, try a chutney instead. This delicious condiment uses two cups of tomatoes and only takes ten minutes to whip up. As a benefit, this also uses up a lot of your herbs, which will go bad if you don't use them quickly. It's great on a hamburger or as a twist on a taco.

Ingredients

2 C tomatoes, chopped

1 T white sugar

2 T cilantro, chopped

1 T ginger, ground

1 T garlic, minced

½ tsp. chili powder

Salt

Instructions

Heat all ingredients in a saucepan

Simmer over medium heat 10 minutes or until thick

Infused Liqueurs

My grandfather was from Yugoslavia. The first drink I ever had was slivovitz, a plum brandy, which he made using plums from his trees. We drank it anytime we had a celebration. And my German grandmother would drink kümmel, a caraway seed brandy. It sounds weird, but it was delicious. That was my introduction to drinks, and infused liqueurs have always been my favorites.

Herbs, fruits, a quart mason jar, and alcohol can make you a kitchen alchemist. Turning a bottle of vodka into something personal and customized is fun to do! Using what you have on hand from your garden is always best. Vodka, being tasteless, takes on whatever flavor is infused into it. Other alcohols can be used, such as rum, whiskey, tequila, or gin. Each will completely change the flavor profile.

Making liqueurs is a social thing—make them as gifts or share with guests. The homemade taste is better than anything on the shelves of the liquor store.

Rose petals

Lemongrass, lemon balm, lemon verbena

Spearmint, peppermint, mint

Orange or lemon peel swirls

Lavender

Cucumber, basil, apples, pears, strawberries, lime, pineapple, jalapeno...the list is endless!

Quart-size jar with lid

Ingredients

Alcohol

Instructions

Grab a few mason jars and find a few flavors you would like to try. Combinations are fun, such as strawberry and vanilla in vodka, whiskey with cranberry and orange, tequila with lime and jalapeno, or rum with strawberry and pineapple.

Most fruit infusions take three to five days to be ready. Herbal infusions can be ready in two days—but they can be potent, so don't overdo the jar. And you only need one day for jalapeno or other spicy flavors. Check the infusion after two days to see if it's done.

Seal and store in a dark place. Your unique infusion can last a long time. When ready, strain and enjoy. When using fruit, the alcohol will keep it safe from mold.

Kahlua

This recipe is a bit of a labor of love, requiring a stir every 15 minutes for 3 hours. I set the timer, and it goes quickly. I have used different rums, even vodka, but in the end, the richness of the Myers's® rum makes all the difference. Bakers know this is the preferred rum to use for baking creations as well. I love creating my own bottles, giving them as gifts, or bringing them out for after-dinner drinks with friends. It's a treat!

INGREDIENTS

4 C water

1 C instant coffee crystals

2 C light brown sugar

2 C dark brown sugar

1 750-ml Myers's® rum or 100-proof vodka

2 tsp. vanilla extract

1 vanilla bean, cut lengthwise and halved

INSTRUCTIONS

In a medium-large pot, combine coffee and water

Bring to a boil

Stir in light and dark brown sugars, reduce heat

Simmer for 3 hours, stirring every 15 minutes

Remove from heat and completely cool

Pour the coffee mixture into a clean ½ gallon mason jar

Add the bottle of Myers's rum into the jar

Add vanilla extract and vanilla bean pieces

Cover and set in a dark place

Shake a few times a week for 1 month

Divide into bottles, putting a piece of vanilla bean in each

Limoncello

This is a spectacularly fun after-dinner drink. I find, however, that I can enjoy it at any time with friends. It's important to use organic lemons so that no pesticides are absorbed as it steeps. Limoncello is made in Italy with Sorrento lemons, but Meyer lemons would be my second choice. The citrus flavor of Sorrento lemons is strong, as limoncello should be; other lemons can fall flat. After peeling, use the remaining whole lemons for other recipes, freezing, or juicing.

Keep at least one bottle of finished limoncello in the freezer so you always have one on hand, ready to serve! Enjoy!

INGREDIENTS

10-14 organic Sorrento lemons

1 750-ml bottle of either Everclear or 80-proof vodka

3½ C filtered water

3 C granulated sugar

1 sprig of rosemary

Simple Syrup

3½ C water

3 C sugar per 750-ml bottle

Heat water on high heat to boiling, then remove from heat

Slowly add sugar, return to heat, and whisk until it returns to a boil

When sugar is dissolved (approx. 2 minutes), take off heat and cool

INSTRUCTIONS

Wash lemons and peel into thin strips, scraping away the white bitter pith with a vegetable peeler

Add lemon peels and rosemary sprig to a ½-gallon mason jar (or any large glass container)

Add vodka

Close the jar lid and shake daily for 4 weeks (the longer, the better)

After 4 weeks, make the simple syrup infusion and pour into the jar of vodka/lemon peel mixture

Close lid and shake

Important

Let jar set for 24 hours after adding simple syrup

Strain out the peels and rosemary sprig with a mesh strainer or sieve

Pour into clean bottles and seal

Sangria

This drink is so much lighter than a typical sangria, and a fun option in the summer or with a Mexican dinner. Sangria can have many fruit combinations, but this seems to be the one everyone loves!

INGREDIENTS

2 peaches, cut in quarters with pit removed

1 orange, cut in quarters

1 C cherries, pitted

⅓ C super-fine sugar

½ C triple sec

1 bottle blush or rose wine

Ice

Optional: seltzer or club soda

INSTRUCTIONS

Add all the ingredients in a large container

Mix, stir, and refrigerate for 1 hour

When ready to serve, pour into pitcher, add ice and edible flowers (or add ice cubes with edible flowers)

As a lighter option, add sparkling water to the sangria

Kümmel

Grandma used this for stomachache, pains, and digestion!

INGREDIENTS

2 T caraway seeds, crushed

1 T fennel seeds, crushed

1 T ground cumin

3 C vodka

2 C sugar

1 C water

INSTRUCTIONS

Combine caraway seed, fennel seed, cumin, and vodka in a jar

Cover tightly and let steep for 2 weeks in a cool dark place, shaking occasionally

When the steeping period is done, strain and filter the liquid

Combine sugar and water in a heavy saucepan

Bring to a boil over medium heat

Reduce heat and simmer until sugar has been completely dissolved, about 3 minutes

Remove from heat and cool to room temperature

Combine sugar syrup and filtered vodka mixture

Pour into bottles and cap tightly

Let age at least 1 month

About the Author

Katie Namet teaches about potager gardening and sustainability around the world. In addition to authoring *The Potager Gardener*, she has written articles, blogs, and videos on potager gardening and cooking, all available on the website she hosts, ThePotagerGardener.com. Katie's e-book, *Vegan Health Lifestyle*, is also offered on her website and helps people understand vegan choices while encouraging healthier food choices with recipe offerings.

Growing up in Chicago, Katie's grandparents were an integral part of her journey. She was captivated by the stories of her European ancestors, their lives on the farm, and how we can incorporate that living anywhere today, even in the city! Intrigued by the idea of finding food sustainability and aesthetic beauty all in one place, she began gardening in an old way called "potager gardening."

From creating all-natural healing products including soaps, lotions, ointments, and medicinal teas, making and selling her own products became a part of Katie's daily life. As a vegetarian on and off in the '90s, she committed fully to the lifestyle. Becoming vegan then required another whole new way of life, with more variety in nutrition. The potager garden fulfilled both business and personal needs, allowing her to grow herbs, flowers, vegetables, and fruits. It's shopping from your garden!

Katie now resides in the Blue Ridge Mountains of North Carolina enjoying all the beauty and exploring all the possibilities she can handle. Her love for nature continues to grow with her experiences in the beautiful south she now calls home.

For more information visit ThePotagerGardener.com.

Printed in the USA
CPSIA information can be obtained
at www.ICGtesting.com
LVHW072342261023
762232LV00016B/191